A Jewish Conservative Looks at Pagan America

A Jewish Conservative Looks at Pagan America

by Don Feder

Huntington House Publishers

Huntington House Publishers
P.O. Box 53788
Lafayette, Louisiana 70505

Library of Congress Card Catalog Number
92-73280
Hardcover ISBN 1-56384-037-5
Quality Trade Paper ISBN 1-56384-036-7

Dedication

This book is dedicated to my parents,
Esther Ruth Feder and Harold Samuel Feder.
In gratitude, which words alone can never
adequately express.

Contents

INTRODUCTION   9

Chapter 1   Family   19

Chapter 2   Faith   43

Chapter 3   Homosexuality   67

Chapter 4   New Age/Humanism/Paganism   75

Chapter 5   Morality/Sexuality   89

Chapter 6   Judaism   105

Chapter 7   AIDS/Sex Education   125

Chapter 8   Media   133

Chapter 9   Drugs/Crime   151

Chapter 10   Pornography   165

Chapter 11   Abortion/Euthanasia   175

Chapter 12   Feminism   203

Chapter 13   Culture   217

Contents

PART ONE

Chapter 1
Chapter 2
Chapter 3
Chapter 4
Chapter 5
Chapter 6

Chapter 7
Chapter 8
Chapter 9
Chapter 10
Chapter 11
Chapter 12

Introduction

This book is a down payment on a debt that can never be fully repaid. For four generations, America has bestowed its blessings on my family. My maternal grandfather (may he rest in peace) arrived here a penniless immigrant at the turn of the century, fleeing oppression in Czarist Russia.

A tailor by trade, he peddled needles and thread door-to-door to earn passage for his family. Here he found religious freedom, a society without class distinctions, an escape from the grinding poverty of ghetto and *shtetl*. His grandchildren include a journalist and a judge, his great-grandchildren a physician and an Orthodox rabbi.

I myself am a child of this century, born practically at midpoint (1946). The most cataclysmic struggle in the course of human history, in which my father took part, was over barely a year. The same year, in a speech at Fulton Missouri, Winston Churchill—a man whose life is a constant source of inspiration for me—marked the onset of the Cold War, a struggle which would involve most of mankind over the next forty-five years.

It was my great good fortune to grow up in a small town in the Mohawk Valley of upstate New York during the 1950s, an era of relative sanity, particularly compared to that which followed.

I was educated in the public schools—by old-maid teachers—when their primary purpose was still the inculcation of knowledge and virtue (the development of faculties, both intellectual and moral), rather than socialization and indoctrination.

At college during the 1960s, I witnessed the fraying of the social fabric, as Dionysian savages built bonfires of traditions, manners, and mores (everything that makes civilization possible), capering about the flames, demonic grins on their countenances.

The seeds sown during the era of do-your-own-thing germinated over the next quarter-century, bearing a bumper crop of poisonous fruit. For the past decade, I've chronicled that madness in my syndicated column. To paraphrase Lincoln Steffens, I have seen the future, and it's given me a massive migraine.

A word about the title of this book. By *Pagan America*, I do not mean the New Age movement, those crystal-caressing shaman in psychobabble trappings, or the sad creatures who proudly proclaim themselves neo-pagans (without the vaguest idea of the ultimate implication of that avowal), though both play a part in the unfolding drama and are considered in this volume.

By *Pagan America* I mean that this is no longer a Judeo-Christian nation, animated by the ethical vision of the Bible, with its special emphasis on honesty, hard work, caring, and self-discipline. Instead we are evolving into the type of Canaanite culture (unrestrained hedonism, ritual prostitution, child sacrifice and the civic virtue of Sodom), which my ancestors encountered at the dawn of moral history.

I observed with sad amusement the furor several years ago when a hapless conservative leader declared that America was a Christian nation, inciting the intense agitation of a near hysterical establishment. By this he was not suggesting that the United States either had or required an official religion, comparable to the Church of England, or that the machinery of government should be harnessed to the propagation of religious dogma.

His statement was a recognition of certain historical/social realities: that America was founded by individuals inspired by the biblical worldview, that most Americans at least pay lip service to those concepts, while many still order their existence by the same, that our national survival depends on the triumph of those values whose proponents are locked in a fierce competition with their opposite number.

The establishment can rest easy. Thanks to its good offices, this is no longer a Christian (or Judeo-Christian) nation. More's the pity. The paganizing of America, a process commenced in the Sixties (but whose intellectual antecedents can be traced back decades) is already well advanced.

A nation will have one God or many. Ours is increasingly polytheistic. While 40 percent of us attend church or synagogue services on Saturday or Sunday (the highest percentage in the industrialized world), the God of Israel isn't among the deities worshiped on weekdays.

The gods of late twentieth century America include the doctrines of radical autonomy, of absolute rights divorced from responsibilities, of gender sameness, of self-expression which acknowledges no higher purpose, of moral relativism and sexual indulgence. Their temples are courtrooms, legislative chambers, classrooms, news rooms, and the executive suites of entertainment conglomer-

ates and publishing firms. We are one nation under God no more.

If my book could be summed up in a single
sentence it would be this: Ideas have consequences.
First the elite, then to a lesser extent (impercepti-
bly, almost subconsciously), the masses embrace
certain toxic notions. The consequences fill our
prisons, drug rehab centers, divorce courts, shel-
ters for the battered and abused, rape crisis centers, mental hospitals, singles bars, and the roster
of guests on the "Oprah Winfrey Show."

In the richest, freest, most tolerant nation on
earth, the impoverishment of the spirit has led to
a values depression. We have enough social pa-
thologies to occupy every medical faculty in the
land for an eon: family dissolution, the flight from
parental responsibility, extramarital sexuality, an
illegitimacy crisis (a situation where 60 percent of
minority children are born out-of-wedlock), a sex-
and-violence saturated "entertainment" media,
drug abuse (an ancient vice corroding the soul of
a modern society), an under class mired in misery,
rampant crime, venomous race relations, labor
that has lost its meaning, and the futile pursuit of
pleasure replacing virtue as our greatest ambition.

When the United States Supreme Court in
effect declares that it's unconstitutional to read
the Declaration of Independence at a high school
graduation, due to its multiple references to the
deity, you can gauge the success of the crusade to
expunge Judeo-Christian ethics from the public
sector.

When a public school teacher may describe
the most bizarre sex acts, in the crudest detail, but
it's considered the mutilation of the first amendment to post the Ten Commandments on a class-

room bulletin board, when a ten-year-old is told that if she quietly reads her Bible on a school bus it is tantamount to the establishment of a national church, we have achieved a society that the Pilgrims, the Founding Fathers, and even our own grandparents would barely recognize.

When celebrities flaunt their illicit relationships, when social organizations like the Boy Scouts are censured and penalized for refusing to bend the knee to immorality, when government tells us that presenting a condom to a thirteen-year-old or giving a needle to an addict is an act devoid of moral content, when the governor of a major industrial state declares that post-viability abortions (i.e. infanticide) is the price we have to pay for freedom, when politicians openly court the votes of degenerates, when a court rules that a sex killer has a constitutional right to his collection of violent pornography—we are on the verge of moral collapse.

When a rap song that calls for the murder of cops climbs to the top of the charts, when taxpayers are told that their objections to subsidizing a photograph of one man urinating into the mouth of another constitute censorship (when critics consecrate the same as the highest expression of the aesthetic), when a state's voters come within a hair's breadth of legalizing medical murder in the name of relieving suffering, when madams tout their memoirs on television talk shows, when a presidential candidate informs voters that whether or not he violated his marriage vows is none of their business, we may as well declare intellectual bankruptcy and have the nation placed in moral receivership.

When eminent authorities tell us that between

the one who gave it life and a total stranger it
makes absolutely no difference who raises a child,
when the law takes the position that parents have
no legitimate interest in whether or not their fifteen-year-old daughters have abortions (in the same
jurisdiction where parental approval is required
for a school nurse to dispense aspirin), when commentators can look at the devastation wrought in
the inner cities by fatherless children and pro-
nounce the problem a paucity of welfare spending, when we are informed that playing with toy
guns warps the psyche but pornography has no
effect on character development—hope fades to a
glimmer.

Pray, do not tell me that America is now a
pluralistic society, that it is impossible to speak of
values when there are so many value-systems to
which the public adheres. That many of our fellow
Americans tacitly reject the Judeo-Christian ethic
is a cause for lamentation not resignation. I'm not
impressed by a variety of life philosophies, but by
value systems that work, that lead to social stabil-
ity, contentment, justice, dignity and cause us (in
the words of the Haggadah—the Passover prayer
book) not to want for any good thing.

Over the past decade, I've written and spoken on a broad range of political issues including
economics, defense, and foreign policy. The focus
of this book is social issues, the moral questions
which have vexed us for a generation and more.

On such things the fate of a civilization hinges.
We can have the strongest economy in the world,
America can achieve strategic superiority which
verges on global hegemony, and it will all be for
naught if we lose our moral bearings. Not that we
could have either a strong economy or the will

to defend ourselves without healthy social institutions, the family first and foremost among them.

My friend Gary Bauer, domestic policy advisor of the Reagan White House, currently head of the Family Research Council, speaks of a cultural civil war raging across the nation. William Bennet, former Secretary of Education, ex-head of the Office of Drug Policy, employs the same concept in his recent book *The De-Valuing of America.*

An apt metaphor this. Arrayed on one side is society's cultural elite (those who command the nation's idea generators): the professoriate, the media (news and entertainment), most elected officials, the bureaucracy, corporate America (when it deigns to take sides), the mainline Protestant churches as well as most foundations.

On the other side are a handful of family activists, social conservatives, a definite minority in academia, a few embattled officeholders, and iconoclastic commentators. Engagements are fought in editorial pages, in high school and college classrooms, and legislative hearing rooms, as well as on TV/radio talk shows. Territory is gained or lost at polling places. The prize is the soul of middle America.

This volume—dispatches from the trenches—covers the most controversial aspects of a debate whose outcome will determine whether the paganizing of America will proceed apace or if, as a society, we will rediscover traditional values: life issues (abortion, euthanasia, fetal tissue experimentation), sexual morality (gay rights, AIDS, sex education, condom distribution, pornography, date rape, sexual harassment, unwed mothers), religion in the public sector (school prayer, the public display of religious symbols, decline of the mainline churches, Evangelicals, Catholics, the New Age movement, neo-pagans), media and culture (the National Endowment for the Arts, sex and violence in entertainment, the negative portrayal of religion and the family therein, nihilism as music), and the family (divorce, day care, drugs, child abuse, elder abuse, population control, masculinity and femininity, educational indoctrination).

The book also presents columns and speeches which examine contemporary problems from a distinctly Jewish perspective: Judaism and abortion, the moral message of the Jewish holidays, an analysis of religion in the public sector, Judaism and homosexuality, Jews and the *Last Temptation of Christ*, and the Jewish mission to humanity.

Taken together, these columns and articles, published between 1984 and 1992, constitute the first social conservative statement from a Jewish perspective—other than Leviticus, of course.

My conservatism rests not on a passion for economic liberty, though I do believe the free market is the most efficient supplier of human needs as well as the only moral system of wealth creation. Nor is it a celebration of European culture, much as I appreciate the contributions of the West in this regard. It does not involve blind allegiance to a nation state, though I will state unequivocally that America's greatness is deserved. It isn't a democratic credo, though—in my estimation—democracy is infinitely preferable to the totalitarian systems which have afflicted humanity so grievously in this century.

My conservatism is God-centered, premised on a passion to nurture the best in human nature, which flows from our acceptance of divine injunctions. It is based on the ethical worldview of the patriarchs and prophets, grounded in the heritage of a people who first taught humanity to think in moral terms.

Conservative Protestants and Catholics loyal to Rome will feel completely at home with this perspective. After all, our values derive from the same source. We learned them together at the foot of a mountain in the Sinai peninsula. I want Christians to know that there are Jews (not Jews by birth, but Jews by conviction) who are every bit as anguished as they over the moral decline of this nation.

The thoughts expressed herein were controversial when first published. They will be no less so in the present format. I expect this book to be reviled by reviewers, its facts disputed, analysis rejected, and motivation questioned.

Still, if it inspires the uninvolved, provides intellectual armament to those grappling on the field of combat, heartens those who look at contemporary society and despair (if only by letting them know that others share their profound misgivings), serves as a call to battle for the ethical majority, I will be well satisfied.

Among the gifts America has given me are four wonderful children. This book was written in the hope that they and their children will someday inherit the America in which I grew up, instead of the nation it has become.

—Boston, Massachusetts, 4 October 1992

ONE

Family

Divorce '90s-style no bed of roses
(12 January 1990)

The most popular movie of the season is a dark look at the devastation of divorce.

War of the Roses is a wickedly black comedy about the perils of uncoupling. It's a tale told by a cynic—family friend and the husband's divorce lawyer—played by actor Danny DeVito, who offers sardonic commentary on the mad proceedings. ("What do you call five hundred lawyers at the bottom of the ocean? A good beginning.")

Roses describes the lengths to which two property-obsessed people will go to protect their sacred possessions. In the course of the film, the yuppie protagonists literally demolish their beautiful home, and themselves, in the process of severing the bonds of matrimony.

The movie's popularity may be due in part to our collective disillusionment with the divorce ethic, the growing recognition that it represents not individual liberation from an oppressive relationship but a personal tragedy with serious societal repercussions.

19

Since 1960, the divorce rate has doubled. A marriage formed today has no more than a 50 percent chance of survival, about the same as a Stalinist in Eastern Europe. It's estimated that half of the children born in the 1980s will spend part of their childhood with only one of their natural parents.

Forget abuse, abandonment, and infidelity; since divorce law "reform" of the 60s, the itchy partner can terminate a relationship for such profound grievances as boredom, rancor, or personality clashes, all included under the rubric "irreconcilable differences."

War of the Roses depicts trench warfare—the bloody, hand-to-hand (take-no-prisoners) combat of the divorce process. In real life, greater problems come after the property settlement and the provision for support and visitation have been granted.

More than any other single factor, divorce is responsible for the feminization of poverty in the past 20 years. In 1983, 54 percent of single-parent, mostly female-headed, households were below the poverty line.

Sociologist Lenore Weitzman discloses that a woman's standard of living will decline 73 percent within a year of divorce. Of the divorced women she surveyed, 70 percent report constant anxiety about "making ends meet" or "not being able to pay bills."

If a woman over forty divorces, her chances of remarriage are comparable to those of being killed by a terrorist. Even younger women with children often are doomed to decades of near poverty, loneliness, and the frustration of solo parenting.

But the financial consequences of divorce are small change compared to the psychic impact. In Judith Wallerstein's study of divorced women over forty, half were clinically depressed, all moderately to severely lonely, notwithstanding that a majority had initiated the process. Divorced men who don't remarry are far more susceptible to mental illness, suicide, and physical ailments than their married counterparts.

Only in movies does the belligerence end when the couple parts company. According to another survey, even ten years after divorce, one-third of the men and half of the women are still "intensely angry with their ex-spouse." There's more than a kernel of truth in the lyrics of the popular country-western ditty: "All my exes live in Texas. That's why Tennessee's my home."

Statistics explode the myth that divorce offers a magical second chance for happiness. The survival rate for second marriages is a mere 30 percent. On the third attempt, the odds of success decline to 15 percent.

All of which prompted psychologist Diane Medved, author of *The Case Against Divorce*, to observe: "I discovered in my research that the process and aftermath of divorce is so pervasively disastrous—to the mind, body and spirit—that in an overwhelming number of cases, the 'cure' that it brings is surely worse than the marriage's disease."

While the victims of divorce come in many sizes, the small ones surely are the most pathetic. During adolescence, children from broken homes are more likely to be promiscuous, abuse alcohol and drugs, suffer from mental illness, and do poorly in school than those from a stable environment.

Nor does the affliction end with adulthood. The cover story in the 29 May 1989 issue of *People* magazine, "Children of Divorce: Wounded Hearts," examined the enduring pain of what is for many the most traumatic experience in their lives.

It once was thought that, given love and support, children would quickly rebound from family dissolution. As the magazine demonstrates in a series of profiles, individuals whose parents divorced when they were in grade school are still feeling the effects into their twenties and thirties. These include fear of commitment, lack of direction, and the feeling that they have little control over their lives. Divorce is no bed of roses. We've made marital break-up far too easy and respectable, and in so doing we have promoted a trend with dire consequences. In this war, society is the ultimate casualty.

Fleeing Parenthood:
Kids do, after all, mess up things
(8 September 1986)

The baby boom of the Forties and Fifties has become the baby bust of the Eighties, according to *Newsweek*, that ubiquitous chronicler of cultural trends.

In a cover story in the Sept. 1 issue, *Newsweek* hails the childless. "But more and more couples are painting a new kind of American family portrait—one with just two faces, the husband's and wife's," the publication enthuses.

Tragically, it is correct. In 1960, only 13 percent of married women (ages 25 to 29) were childless. Today 29 percent of women in that age group are *sans* children. In 1965, 16 percent of married couples were voluntarily sterile. Their numbers have risen to 39 percent.

The magazine offers stock excuses for this dramatic flight from parenthood. Women are no longer satisfied with traditional roles, preferring the mythic fulfillment of careers to dealing with diapers and juvenile ailments.

The cost of raising a kid is daunting, *Newsweek* informs us—as much as $135,000 from cradle to college. Most revealing are the comments of a professor of civil engineering, quoted in the article, who admits: "I like to do things for myself. I'm just not ready to sacrifice my time to a kid."

The trendies interviewed for the story concur: kids are inconvenient, messy, time-consuming, and a detraction from hot-tubish pleasures of the quiche crowd.

A scruffy young man, who works for a Chicago medical center, refuses to bring a child into a world poised on the brink of a nuclear apocalypse, as he puts it. Besides, a youngster would interfere with political commitments, preventing him and his activist spouse from flying off to Central American trouble spots for protest weekends.

An executive with a Wall Street firm dreads the thought of a child spoiling the ivory silk upholstery on her living room couch. "I enjoy what I'm doing," she muses. "Having children isn't going to buy me more contentment." In the yuppie universe, ultimately everything is related to its gratification-conferring potential.

"I find the whole idea of pregnancy repugnant . . . I'm not wild about children," declares a Boston-based writer, pictured with her husband playing with a bubble wand. One can only thank Providence that certain perpetual adolescents won't reproduce.

The magazine is very much on the side of the childless-by-choice. A study is noted which purports to show that families without kids are happier than their parenting counterparts. A mother remarks that those who choose not to have offspring "may take the responsibility of parenting more seriously than couples who simply take the plunge because it's expected."

The villain in this scenario, *Newsweek* discloses, is the cultural attitude (designated a legacy of the 1950s) which attempts to pressure people into child-bearing. The article casts a fleeting glance at thunderclouds on the population horizon. The decline in procreation, combined with better health care, is giving us an increasingly older citizenry. Who will support the retirees of the next century?

The American birthrate currently is below replacement level. Given this trend and the Third World population explosion, how will America maintain its civilization and position as a world power? A century hence, perhaps developing nations will be the first world, and we the third.

The urge to child-avoidance runs much deeper than the rationalizations *Newsweek* offers. Child-rearing is an act of love. Many moderns are too wrapped up in themselves, too self-infatuated, to have affection to spare for another human being.

It is also a life-affirming act. Parenthood is an affirmation of a belief in the goodness of existence, of our love for life and the world around us. Valuing life, we symbolically declare our desire that humanity continue after us.

Thus having a child ultimately is a spiritual act, a recognition of order in the universe and purpose to existence. Hardly surprising, then, that procreation is the earliest biblical commandment.

Abstention from parenting is related to a general lessening of faith. In assisting in the generation of human life, parents not only fulfill a religious obligation, but come as close as possible to imitating the Creator.

In the remake of the movie *Scarface*, the immigrant gangster contemptuously dismisses his coke-snorting wife with the observation that her body is too polluted to produce a baby. The rise of voluntary childlessness is yet another symptom of the modern malaise. A poisoned tree bears no fruit. Similarly, a civilization corrupted with narcissism, skepticism, and secularism will yield a declining crop of society's most important product.

There are compensations in parenthood, that accrue as one ages, which today's childless couples will never know. Who will be there to comfort them in their declining years? Who will mourn them? Instead of grandchildren, they can hug their silk-upholstered couches.

Big families are socially responsible
(24 October 1991)

It was "the most socially responsible thing I've done in a long time," trilled *Washington Monthly* contributing editor Scott Shuger of his vasectomy. A paladin of population control, Shuger put his reproductive organs on the line and now preens for our approval.

He's so darned proud of his personal contribution to the cause, that he just had to tell all in an article ("Kindest Cut: My vasectomy—and yours?") in the Oct. 14 *New Republic*.

"An alarming . . . 40 percent of births in this country result from unintended pregnancy," Shuger breathlessly informs us. Horrors, imagine—life happening spontaneously! (Nature can be so messy.) The fault lies with men, he confesses in a spasm of new-mannish gender guilt. We are "birth control wimps."

Based on his personal experience, Shuger is so high on cut, cut—snip, snip that he urges a campaign on the scale of Desert Storm to persuade men that sterile-is-beautiful, including "aggressive outreach" and more bucks for woefully underfunded family planning programs. After all, sex education and contraceptive expenditures only increased twenty-fold (from $13.5 million to $279 million) between 1969 and 1979.

The piece ends in an orgy of new male-bonding, as Shuger describes his cheerful banter with the medics who fixed him. Ah, the joys of Nineties manhood.

There are a number of unstated premises here, to which the author alludes with his self-congratulatory pat on the social conscience: that America is in imminent danger of being buried under the debris from a detonating population bomb, that too many people will capsize spaceship earth, that "unwanted" children are an awful burden.

Before pushing the panic button, it's important to understand what is meant by an "unplanned pregnancy." According to the population controllers, unless a child is desired by both partners at the point of conception (never mind how they feel later), it's an unplanned pregnancy, hence a serious social concern.

Did Mr. and Mrs. Washington "plan" their fifth child, the one who grew up to be our first president? In a culture obsessed with arranging every detail of existence (education, career, retirement, even leisure pursuits) the unintended is ominous. America's demographic problem in the next century won't be a population glut but a birth dearth. Our birthrate has hovered just below replacement level for the past two decades, plunging from 3.77 children per woman in 1957 to 2.0 today. The nation's birthrate is actually lower now than in 1944, when 7,447,000 young men were serving overseas.

Evidence of the empty cradle crisis may be seen in the graying of our nation, the schools transformed into senior housing, the baby clothes manufacturers scaling back their operations while pharmaceutical firms, whose profits rest with seniors, enjoy an unprecedented boom.

As Thomas Fleming notes in the October issue of *Chronicles*, the population control visionaries "refuse to distinguish between the American middle class and the beggars of Calcutta." The former fire an industrial engine which produces a quarter of the world's manufactured goods.

Regrettably, the people least likely to heed Shuger's call to social responsibility are residents of Third World ant heaps and the seventeen-year-old unwed mother with her teeming welfare brood, not to mention her bevy of unemployed boyfriends.

Those most susceptible to the call to class

suicide, through guilt or misperceived self-interest, are nice suburban couples. The children they never had might have grown up to write a symphony, develop a revolutionary manufacturing process, or find a cure for daytime television.

An industrial civilization can't be maintained without people. The population rise of the modern era paved the way for the industrial revolution of the late eighteenth and early nineteenth centuries.

Because our parents and grandparents chose to have large families, we can enjoy the amenities of modern America, giving us the opportunity to neglect our procreative duties for career advancement, two-paycheck families, and a dazzling array of pleasures.

But what will come after us? How will today's demographic drought support a comparable living standard for future generations? If you have the means to support them, and the values to raise them well, having a large family is the most socially responsible thing you can do.

More significantly, procreation is a celebration of life. To voluntarily relinquish the ability to create life makes a profound statement of regard for the same. It also bespeaks a loss of faith, an insistence that we, and not our Maker, know best when it comes to determining family size. How well the psalmist put it (Psalm 127:3-5): "Behold, children are a gift of the Lord; the fruit of the womb is a reward. Like arrows in the hands of a warrior, so are the children of one's youth."

In a way it's fitting that an increasingly sterile culture of plastic values and throw-away relationships would embrace contraception with almost religious fervor.

'Abuse' not always what it seems to be
(2 April 1989)

Joel Steinberg, who killed his six-year-old illegally adopted daughter, is going away for a long time, but not long enough. His sentencing provoked another outpouring of expert opinion, so-called, on the subject of child abuse—much of it hazardous to the health of American families.

On the day sentence was pronounced, Dr. Eli Newberger, a physician on the staff of Boston's Children's Hospital and a member of a newly-created state task force on child abuse, confided that the problem cuts across socio-economic lines. ("Disclosures of sexual abuse appear to be particularly prevalent in affluent homes.")

Like many professionals in the area, Dr. Newberger seeks an ever-expanding definition of child abuse. In his estimation, spanking is a form of violence to children which must be carefully monitored and prosecuted at the first sign of a bruise. The message of the Steinberg case, the doctor gravely pronounces, is that "most child abusers look just like you and me." So as soon as you see anything suspicious, folks, grab that phone and report your neighbors to the appropriate social service agency.

Need it be said? Joel Steinberg and Hedda Nussbaum are hardly Ozzie and Harriet. Joel was a drug lawyer, coke head, and sadist (who freebased cocaine as his daughter lay dying); Hedda, his unmarried mate, gave new dimensions to the term masochistic. If this sounds like the folks next-door to you, I suggest you consider relocating, posthaste.

Has child abuse reached epidemic levels? It's certainly in the interest of the child abuse industry to make us believe so. Their shock in trade is citing alarming statistics: i.e., 2.1 million cases reported in 1986. They neglect to note that 60 percent of all reports prove to be unfounded. Even that figure overstates the situation, as zealous social workers often stretch the criteria to fit any family believed to be in need of "intervention."

The view that child abuse is rife among intact middle-class families is ludicrous. Douglas Besharov, former director of National Center on Child Abuse and Neglect, states: "Families reported for maltreatment are four times more likely to be on public assistance" than the general population. Researchers at Canada's McMaster University established that in 1985 "preschoolers living with one natural and one stepparent were 40 times more likely to become child abuse cases than were like-aged children living with two natural parents."

Sexual abuse prevalent among ordinary families? Not according to political scientist Jean Bethke Elshtain who discloses that: "In two-thirds of all cases of father-daughter incest, the offender is not a biological parent but a step-father or live-in roommate of the mother." In other words, if child abuse is indeed on the rise, it was fostered by welfare, easy divorce, and single-parent families—endowments of the same ideology which now proclaims its intention to combat the crisis by massive intrusion in the American family.

Almost any excuse for intervention is seized upon. Writing in the *New York Times*, Susan Pouncey urges us to eliminate child abuse by banning corporal punishment. Imagine having the cops batter down your door because a neighbor saw you give your child a swat on the behind?

I went to college in the Sixties with kids who were raised by the book—Dr. Spock's baby book. Their parents never spanked them, rarely raised their voices in anger. A more obnoxious bunch of spoiled brats I hope never to meet. Political violence and the drug culture were their temper tantrums.

Emotional abuse is the latest just-discovered contagion, even worse than physical abuse the experts say (leaves psychological scars that never heal, don't you know). The day is not far off when yelling at little Yolanda, as she attempts to flambé the family cat, will have the child abuse hot line ringing off the wall.

Where might all of this lead? In a 1988 issue of *Family Law Quarterly*, Claudia Pap Mangel proposes licensing parents as the most efficient way to check violence against children. Prospective parents would need state certification before they're allowed to procreate. Winston Smith, your sizeable sibling is calling.

Day care workers are busy hatching a brave new world
(4 March 1991)

For years, Americans have agonized over the potential effects of institutionalized child care. Day care advocates told them it was okay to leave infants and toddlers with total strangers for eight to ten hours a day. But almost intuitively they seemed to know that the cost of day care would be paid not just in dollars and cents but in their children's emotional well-being.

Not to worry, America. Now comes day-care worker Jane Palzere with glad tidings: Collective child-rearing isn't merely an adequate substitute but is actually far superior to parental care.

Writing in the *Hartford Courant*, Palzere admits that she was one of those neurotic, guilt-ridden Sixties moms who stayed home to raise her brood. "I am amazed at how wrong I was to think that staying home and raising my children was such a noble thing to do." Palzere confesses. Why, if her son had the advantages of kiddie warehousing: "He would have been free to explore, discover, communicate with others his own size out of the presence of a nagging, fretful, and overprotective mother . . .

"Another factor in day care is that babies get total care." she assures us. "There is plenty of cuddling, lots of attention, personal communication . . . things I could not always give my own children . . ."

Leave it to the experts, Palzere advises. "Trained personnel who know what to expect in child development and children's needs far surpass the naive, fumbling new mother."

If, at this point, you're curious about the coordinates of Palzere's home planet, hold on: her article gets infinitely more extraterrestrial. "There is a great deal of beauty in a day-care center," she enthuses. Indeed, they are the incubators of a brave new world. "For as these children grow, knowing that everyone has to work together for the common good, they can . . . bring into the future valuable lessons."

Sounding like a combination of Mary Poppins and Vladimir Lenin, Palzere suggests this social-ization, "might just be the hope of our future." Here is the age-old dream of tyrants: Give me a child for its formative years, and I'll give you back an adult with my values, obedient to my com-mands.

The warm, loving, highly interactive day-care center Palzere describes exists nowhere in the known universe. In the best facilities there is little adult contact, little stimulation, especially for in-fants. The worst are nothing short of nightmarish.

A growing body of data points to the devel-opmental hazards of child care. Writing in the current issue of *Family in America*, J. Craig Peery, former special assistant to the chairman of the U.S. Senate Committee on Labor and Human Resources, summarizes this research, noting that day care kids tend to be more aggressive, less affectionate, and less cooperative with adults than those reared by parents. "Third-graders who were placed in day-care as preschoolers are viewed more negatively by their peers, have lower academic grades, and demonstrate poor study skills."

More than emotional development is at risk. Children in centers are 25 percent more likely to contract colds and diarrhea. For the more serious diseases, including frequently fatal ailments like meningitis, the rate of risk increases 50 to 100 percent for the denizens of day care.

Among the "beautiful things" going on in some day-care centers are physical and sexual abuse. Between 1980 and 1984, complaints about abuse in Texas facilities nearly doubled. In one study of sexual abuse in Michigan, 75 percent of the victims were day-care children.

Though loaded with misinformation and wishful thinking to make Pollyanna seem like a bottom-line businessman, Palzere's piece is most welcome in one regard. Child-care advocates are generally too clever to reveal their hidden agenda.

Imagine Marian Wright Edelman of the Children's Defense Fund announcing: "Hey, Middle America, we want to brainwash your kids. We would destroy their allegiance to your values (archaic concepts like family, religion, patriotism, private property) and inculcate our dogma in their place. We want to mold good, servile little citizens of the welfare state, committed to the secularist worldview."

No, no. That won't do at all. Instead, tell them that women in the work force are a reality (but don't let them ask why) and that something must be done to accommodate them. Say women have an inherent right to a career, that a woman can only be fulfilled by employment outside the home. Say day care won't harm its charges, to the best of our knowledge. But whatever you do, don't get into the philosophy behind the movement.

Frank admissions such as Palzere's are rare—rare but highly revealing. The candor of this day-care champion nearly compensates for her fairy-tale portrayal of the salubrious effects of social strychnine.

There are no time limits on family obligations
(5 February 1990)

Joan France has had it up to here with family ties. Kids and seniors, get out of the way! Joan needs "free time to pursue (her) own happiness."

France voices her frustration in the "My Turn" column of *Newsweek's* Jan. 29 issue. A year ago, her son, age twenty-nine, entered a drug rehabilitation program. When the clinic requested that she participate in his therapy, France flatly refused.

It seemed the little swine had conned her before, and she wasn't about to be taken in again. And even if he really *did* need her, she'd already given quite enough.

She was offended by the assumption that, as his mother, she would willingly contribute to his treatment. "I received no help from the professionals working on my son's case," France whines. Apparently, said professionals didn't sufficiently sympathize with her unwillingness to sacrifice further.

"I have seen one friend after another in great distress over emergencies created by their adult children. They usually get sucked into the mess," France laments. Warming to the theme, she delivers her manifesto: "I want to call a halt to this exploitation of parents. Specifically, I want to sound a warning to my own generation. We are rapidly becoming the caretaker generation."

France is indignant over adult children, selfish beasts that they are, constantly making demands on their parents' emotions, finances, and

time. The "caretakers," moreover, are getting it
from both ends of the generational spectrum.
"Many of us are dealing with peevish elderly parents . . . Some of these old people are demanding
and self-absorbed . . ."

Tragic, is it not? Well, the much-abused
Frances of the world aren't about to take it one
minute longer. "Our spoiled children can face the
consequences of their choices and shoulder their
own responsibilities. Our complaining parents have
other housing options available to them. We want
some peace and some free time to pursue our
own happiness."

May I address a modest query to the "caretaker generation?" If your children are spoiled,
who spoiled them? If they're irresponsible, could
it be because you failed to teach them responsibility?

I have portentous news for defaulting parents: Your responsibility to your progeny didn't
end when they turned eighteen or walked out
your door. You bore them. For better or worse,
they're yours.

As for your parents, what you owe them you
can never repay. A large part of who and what you
are is due to their nurturing. Growing old isn't
pleasant. It hurts, both physically and emotionally. Unless you're a saint, you'll probably be peevish too, as you enter your not-so-golden years.

Those of us who view children not as a biological accident but a gift—and an obligation—from
God are quite clear about this: We didn't sign an
eighteen-year contract with the Almighty.

Under ordinary circumstances, our responsibility to provide food and shelter may be finite.

But our duty to guide, to give of our time, to care is infinite. The contract is open-ended. Similarly, the commandment to honor one's parents does not, as I recall, contain an exclusionary clause for elders who are crotchety, insistent, or unreasonable.

The wonderful—and the awful—thing about families is that (like the mafia, also given to familial metaphors) there's no way out. The ties of blood, of time, of a multitude of shared memories cannot be severed at will.

We may deny their pull, protest that we have given all we can, that we're tired of being bound to these ungrateful offspring and grasping parents. It does no good. Family is destiny. It shapes us in the cradle. We in turn pass on the legacy with our own contributions. How can we deny those who created us—both literally and figuratively—or those whom we created?

What happiness will France find, once annoying seniors have been packed off to the nursing home and errant offspring left to sink in or surmount the difficulties of their own devising? Aerobics classes? Gardening? Cable TV? Macrame?

We may love leisure-time activities, but they (poor things) can't love us back. The most enduring happiness comes from others. In this regard, none can give us more pleasure or pain—more recognition, comfort, and spiritual sustenance—than our families.

Elder abuse tied to devaluation of life
(10 May 1990)

When society signals that the value of human life is relative, the results are always ugly.

Last week a subcommittee of the House Select Committee on Aging released a report which should shock the nation. According to the study, an estimated 1.5 million elderly (one in twenty) are annual victims of abuse, an increase of 500,000 in the past decade.

The report is filled with appalling examples: an elderly woman who weighed sixty pounds and had maggots crawling on an open leg wound when she was brought to a hospital; a sixty-nine-year-old who'd suffered a stroke, found naked, lying on the floor in her own excrement; a man (malnourished and covered with insect bites) tied to his wheelchair; a woman with deep purple bruises on all of the uncovered parts of her body. It's a frightening mosaic of elders beaten, starved, robbed, and neglected by their children.

In examining the origins of the crisis, the report serves up a generous helping of sociological gobbledygook about "unemployment, drug and alcohol abuse and crowded living conditions."

Makes sense, doesn't it? You're out of work, your apartment is too small, so naturally you'll want to burn your aged mother with cigarettes or beat her with a knotted electrical cord.

One medical expert, interviewed on network radio, offered the following rationale: Like children, the elderly are dependent, but instead of being cute and cuddly, they are physically unattractive, thus exciting animosity.

Which, of course, does not explain the battering of the cute and cuddly. According to the National Committee for the Prevention of Child Abuse, in a single year (1988-89), reported cases of child abuse jumped 10 percent, to 2.4 million.

The subcommittee's report comes closer to the truth when it notes: "Sometimes, after parent and child have been separated emotionally or geographically for lengthy periods, the elderly parent's return is viewed as an intrusion." Also, "many middle-aged family members, finally ready to enjoy time to themselves, are resentful of a frail, dependent elderly parent."

In a society oriented toward self-indulgence, the old, the young, the terminally-ill are viewed as intolerable burdens. That which detracts from the *quality* of our lives is often ignored, lashed out at in anger, obliterated.

Every day, in diverse ways, society tells us that certain lives simply are not worth living. When our culture was governed by a religious ethos, all of life was endowed with an aura of sanctity. No more.

Since 1973, nearly 23 million unborn children have been disposed of by women and men who considered their existence inconvenient.

In a March 1989 opinion poll, a plurality said life begins at conception and 62 percent declared that abortion is murder—yet 63 percent concurred that a woman should have an abortion if her doctor agrees. That is to say: (1) It's life, and (2) Terminating it is murder, but (3) It's OK. Only those indoctrinated in the ideology that human life is expendable could simultaneously hold such beliefs.

Each year, at the bequest of their parents, thousands of Down's syndrome babies are deliberately starved to death in hospital nurseries. Courts allow families to remove feeding tubes from comatose patients.

Former Colorado Governor Richard Lamm, the Grim Reaper's publicist, makes explicit what others only suggest. In a 1984 speech, Lamm advised the elderly ill that they have "a duty to die and get out of the way."

They are wasting precious resources, the futurist fumed, wealth which "the other society, our kids [need to] build a reasonable life." Lamm compared seniors who voluntarily refuse extraordinary means to prolong their lives to "leaves falling off a tree and forming humus for other plants to grow up." An interesting metaphor, this. Recall which totalitarian movement turned people into fertilizer and its zeal in disposing of those it deemed unfit to live.

They tell us the elderly are a burden, an unnecessary drain on social assets. ("They're not producing. They'll just die in a few years anyway.") We condone the destruction of inconvenient lives. Medical technology assists it. Political movements (reproductive rights, right-to-die) have sprung up to justify it. Is it any wonder then that the most vulnerable among us increasingly are under attack?

The Ten Commandments are grouped into two general divisions: those that relate to man's obligations to God and those which touch upon his relationship to others. The Fifth Commandment, honor thy father and mother—has traditionally been assigned to the former. Parents were viewed as God's agents on earth, the conduit for His instruction.

The society which turns its back on God, which views individual autonomy and personal gratification as the highest purpose of existence, ultimately will devalue the elderly, our link with eternity.

In your declining years, how will you be viewed by your children: as God's surrogate or a parasitical consumer of scarce resources?

TWO

Faith

Evolution vs. creationism
(21 May 1990)

On the subject of evolution, there is an anecdote about Rabbi Moshe Finestein, the greatest Torah sage of his generation.

On a flight to Tel Aviv, the rabbi was seated next to an Israeli labor leader. Throughout the flight, a girl would periodically approach the rabbi, inquire after his comfort, fluff his pillow, ask if he needed anything.

At last, his curiosity piqued, the union official asked who the child was. "That's my granddaughter," the rabbi replied. The other snorted: "One of my grandchildren wouldn't cross the street for me." "Ah," said the rabbi, "here's the difference. Religious Jews believe that we are all the descendants of Adam. My grandchildren look at me and think: 'He's two generations closer to God's unique creation.'

"You are a secularist and an evolutionist. Your grandchildren look at you and think: 'Two generations closer to the monkey.'"

43

That story came to mind when I saw *Time* magazine's interview with Harvard paleontologist Stephen Jay Gould.

The best-selling author does not hide his disdain for creationists. "They are fairly marginal. They represent but a tiny minority of religious people in America," Gould observes. But when asked if the battle with this fanatical fringe is over, he cautions: "It will never formally end as long as there are millions of them out there with lots of money." Not having read his books, I can't say if such glaring inconsistency (they're a tiny minority, consisting of millions of people) suffuses the body of his work.

The interview was revelatory. Gould agreed with the interviewer that humankind is a "cosmic accident." Under slightly altered circumstances, the mighty evolutionary machine might have produced vastly different results.

Not only are you an accident, but a mishap headed for extinction. According to evolutionist gospel, all creatures are in a constant state of flux, genetic raw material for the next link in the hereditary chain. "If our presence is a fault, what then is the reason for our existence," the interviewer reasonably inquires. To which the noble scientist can only respond: "There is as much reason for us to be here as there is for anything else." In other words, humanity has just as much—but no more—right to inhabit this planet as the cockroach and the toad.

The theory of evolution holds that species and subspecies of the animal kingdom are in constant competition. In the struggle for survival, the successful competitors flourish, the losers go the

way of the brontosaurus and the liberal Demo-
crat.

Darwin believed the same principle could be
applied to the racial and ethnic divisions of humanity. "Looking to the world at no very distant
date, what endless number of *lower races* will have
been eliminated by the higher civilized races
throughout the world," the father of evolutionary
theory predicted. Thomas Huxley, the great man's
arch-disciple, did not doubt the identity of these
inferiors, commenting: "No rational man cognizant of the facts, believes that the average Negro
is the equal . . . of the white man."

In our own century, there has been no shortage of aspirants for the coveted title of
ubermenschen. Adolf Hitler, a devout Darwinian,
believed the Aryan race was best suited for the
intra-species rivalry. "In nature there is no pity for
lesser creatures when they are destroyed so that
the fittest may survive. It is only Jewish impudence which demands that we overcome nature,"
the Fuhrer declared.

Under the Third Reich, Aryan competition
for survival commenced with weeding out defec-
tive members of the race (murdering mental patients and the handicapped) and culminated in
efforts to uproot *inferior* stock, Jews and Slavs.

The other national practitioner of Darwinism
was Josef Stalin. Marx taught him that human
evolution was properly understood not in racial
but class terms. In order to aid the proletariat,
degenerate classes (bourgeoisie, peasant farmers)
were ruthlessly liquidated.

Doubtless, modern proponents of evolution,
such as Gould, are horrified by these political

applications of Darwin's ideology. But how can
they properly oppose them? If humanity is cosmic
happenstance, rather than divinely ordained, how
can they reasonably object to one accident nullify-
ing another? With mankind fathered by biological
chance—headed toward inevitable obsolescence—
how can ethics be anything but relative? The rabbi
was right; theories have consequences.

Religion takes a bashing in the courts
(20 June 1991)

In ancient times, when Norman Vincent Peale
and Bishop Fulton Sheen roamed the earth, religion was treated with the utmost deference. Doctrinal differences notwithstanding, religion was
considered a public good—its practice beneficial
to the moral vitality of the community. This was
reflected in Forties films, with their invariably benevolent priests, magnanimous ministers, and wise
rabbis.

Deference has turned to disdain, particularly
for fundamentalist faiths. We're uncomfortable
around people who take God seriously and are
anxious to segregate them.

Zoning laws are a versatile stratagem here. A
group of Orthodox Jews has filed a federal suit,
charging the incorporation of a village in upstate
New York is an attempt to deny their civil rights.

Orthodox from New York City have been
moving upstate to escape the delights of urban
existence. Some of their neighbors view the move
with alarm. In April, the Village of Airmont incor-
porated in order to repeal a zoning variance which
allows residents of an Orthodox neighborhood to
have a small synagogue in a rabbi's house.

Since the Orthodox can't ride on their Sabbath, they require a synagogue in walking distance of their homes. In establishing the mini-sanctuary, they complied with all existing zoning regulations, fire codes, etc. Their development is a good quarter of a mile from non-Orthodox neighbors.

But the latter find the very presence of the Orthodox somehow offensive. A leader of the incorporation effort is alleged to have told a public meeting that he wanted "to keep those Orthodox from Brooklyn out of here."

What with beards and black hats, Orthodox men do look different. They don't join the PTA or frequent the local McDonald's. Their focus on spiritual concerns makes secular neighbors nervous.

It's a terribly short-sighted attitude. I'd rather live next-door to someone who looked nothing like me, whose religion was light-years removed from my own—a Mormon, a Jehovah's Witness, a Southern Baptist—who nonetheless shared my values, than a Shirley MacLaine crystal-worshipping neo-pagan from my own socio-economic stratum.

Discrimination against the religious is the one respectable form of prejudice left. Far from an establishment of religion, the governmental apparatus has become a bureaucratic *auto-da-fe*, at which the faithful are regularly flambéed.

• Last year a federal district court upheld the authority of a St. Paul suburb to evict a storefront church on the grounds that the area where it had been located for two years is zoned commercial, and a church would contribute to the economic decline of an already depressed district.

Zoning laws then can be used to keep churches out of both residential and commercial areas. What does that leave? Can't put them in rural surroundings. Choir practice might agitate the cows. Dirty little secret: courts have allowed smut shops greater first amendment rights than churches in contesting restrictive zoning.

• The Gospel Lighthouse Church is suing Dallas, arguing a municipal ordinance makes it practically impossible to construct a Christian school in the city. In Dallas, if 20 percent of the neighbors object to the location of a church school, the site must be approved by three-quarters of the city council. One church spent $100,000 in a futile attempt to get a building permit. Naturally, public schools are exempt from the requirement. As each student removed from the public system saves taxpayers an average of $4,800 you'd think promoting religious education would be a public priority.

• An inquisition is underway to remove the vestiges of religion from public education. Under threat of legal action, a Norman, Oklahoma elementary school agreed to let eleven-year-old Monette Rethford read her Bible on the playground. (The case was referred to by Bush in his June 6 speech to the Southern Baptist Convention.) Initially the fifth grader was informed the pernicious practice was a First Amendment violation.

• Sidewalk ministers have been harassed and arrested in a number of cities. The war on drugs? Forget it! Psalm-singing preachers are the real threat to public order.

Maureen Kendrick, the mayor of Airmont, home of the zoning pogrom, resents the implication of bigotry. "I object to the fact that you try to do something for your children and you're labeled an anti-Semite," Kendrick complains.

By what bizarre reasoning does madame la mayor conclude that keeping a house of worship out of her neighborhood—discouraging a group of people who practice the biblical precepts of charity, modesty, and honesty from settling there— will benefit her children?

According to a report released by the surgeon general last week, half-a-million high-school students get drunk each weekend. You think the drug plague is confined to the inner cities, that teen pregnancy is something that doesn't happen to whitebread suburban kids? But never mind, Kendrick and company are on a crusade to save their children from the doleful effects of exposure to religion.

Protecting kids from God
(11 June 1990)

Each month, an estimated 3 million students are victims of in-school crime. The statistic includes 2.5 million robberies and thefts, 282,000 assaults, and 2,500 acts of arson. In the same period, 1,000 teachers sustain injuries—inflicted by their charges—serious enough to require medical attention. Half-a-million students say they're afraid most of the time while in school.

Of those high-school seniors who use cocaine, 57 percent reported "scoring" at school. The average inner-city pupil is safer on the mean streets of his neighborhood than in the classrooms and corridors of the local temple of learning.

Yet with the keenest discernment does the

National Association of State Boards of Education
perceive that it's Bibles, not bullets, which constitute the real threat to our kids. Thus the organization sought to overturn the federal Equal Access
Act, which forbids discrimination against student
religious groups.

In upholding the act last week, the Supreme
Court brushed aside the admonitions of the association and its allies in the ACLU and People for
the American Way that Bible study groups, meeting during periods set aside for extracurricular
activities, represent a flagrant First Amendment
violation. Today, Bible study, tomorrow the Church
of America, Jerry Falwell presiding, as archbishop
of Lynchburg.

Humanists and their bureaucratic allies are
on an ideological search-and-destroy mission, determined to expunge even the mildest manifestations of religious values in public education. They
have had notable successes: a graduating senior in
New Orleans whose valedictory address was cen-
sored because she quoted the words of Christ: the
child who was forbidden to read her Bible on a
school bus; the third-grader who couldn't display
her valentines because they contained the inscription "I love Jesus," the teens who were prohibited
from distributing religious pamphlets on school
grounds.

The Supreme Court encourages this lunacy
by its persistent efforts to determine the number
of celestial beings who can comfortably cavort on
a comma in the establishment clause. Voluntary
school prayer is out, says the institution which
begins its sessions with the supplication that the
Almighty "save this honorable court." Ditto a
moment of silence. Students might be encour-

aged to think about You-Know-Who. Publishers have followed the trend, by excising religious references from texts.

Posting the Ten Commandments is an intolerable display of favoritism toward the ethos on which our nation was founded. Christmas carols are okay, if they're interspersed with "Frosty the Snowman" and other non-sectarian ditties. Likewise, creches may be displayed on public property, as long as they're carefully camouflaged by Santa Clauses, plastic reindeer, and giant candy canes.

Even the Reagan court, so-called, perpetuates the myth that a constitutional provision intended to bar preference to a specific denomination in fact prohibits any spiritual expression in the public sphere.

It has reached the point where public school students can experience anything—things the average sailor on shore leave doesn't encounter—except God. Sex education, suicide studies, life-boat ethics, condom distribution, abortion pleading, highly explicit descriptions of homosexual acts—which, when taken together, constitute the propagation of the humanist creed—all are essential aspects of the public school experience in the 1990s. It's only prayers, Bibles, and references to a supreme being which offend the sensibilities of secularist puritans.

Please note which side employs coercion to advance its cause, the same which insists that refusing to subsidize obscene art is a form of censorship. No one is suggesting that children be forced to pray or compelled to profess beliefs which run contrary to their values. It is secularists who make war on conscience. No professions of faith, how-

ever voluntary, no religious activities, however far
removed from institutional auspices, will they tolerate.

We may fail to teach our students the rudi-
ments of literature, science, and history. Twenty
percent of high-school graduates may be functional
illiterates, or semi-literate. We may be unable to
maintain even a semblance of order in our urban
schools, which increasingly resemble happy hour
in Beirut. But, hallelujah, we sure know how to
protect kids from God.

Religion no opiate in the East
(12 November 1990)

It's official. After hostilities spanning the century, the *opiate of the masses* has vanquished the
vanguard of the proletariat. Religion is not only the
chief beneficiary of the revolutionary changes
sweeping the communist world, but the principal
instigator as well.

File the following under I-never-thought-I'd-
live-to-see-the-day. In October, while the nation's
leaders looked on, Patriarch Alexi II led the first
religious services within the walls of the Kremlin
since 1917.

Earlier in the month, the Soviet parliament
passed a freedom of conscience law guaranteeing
a broad range of religious rights, prohibiting state
interference in church affairs, and getting government out of the business of propagating atheism.

The religious renaissance going on within the
Soviet Union makes a Baptist tent meeting look
sedate by comparison: Jewish day schools opening, priests running for public office, clergy ap-
pearing regularly on television to deliver the Sun-

day sermon, one thousand Orthodox churches (confiscated by the state) returned to religious authorities, and Protestants holding revivals in stadiums in Moscow and Leningrad.

This fall, Poland's non-communist government initiated voluntary religion classes in its public schools. Schools which once were centers of atheist indoctrination henceforth will offer spiritual instruction.

Consistently underestimating the power of religion, the U.S. media assumed the revolutions in Eastern Europe were fueled by such mundanities as economics and democracy.

While these certainly played a part in the collapse of communism—people indeed are weary of the stale-bread living standards of proletarian paradise and do want a modicum of control over their lives—there was a more profound agent of change than mere material yearnings.

Solidarity would never have succeeded without the support of the Roman Catholic Church. In this devoutly Catholic nation, priests like the martyred Fr. Popieluszko gave the anti-communist labor movement its moral foundation.

In Romania, the uprising which overthrew the Ceausescu regime was sparked by resistance to the removal of a dissident pastor of the Hungarian Reformed Church. The first bloody clash occurred in Timisoara when several thousand demonstrators physically prevented the Securitate from arresting the Rev. Laszlo Tokes.

Nor is the phenomenon confined to Eastern Europe. In Afghanistan, Mujahedeen went into battle shouting "God is great." When Violeta Chamorro received news of her election as president of Nicaragua, ringing down the curtain on the nation's ten-year Marxist regime, her first act was to lead her followers in saying the Ave Maria.

Even in the heartland of scientific material-ism, religion was the catalyst for a revival of free-dom. Alexandr Solzhenitsyn's writing is animated by an orthodox Christian vision. In prison, dissi-dent Natan Sharansky was sustained by a Hebrew copy of the Book of Psalms. In his first meeting with the pope, Gorbachev casually, but meaning-fully, remarked: "My mother had me baptized in the Orthodox Church."

Communism's inability to eradicate man's spiritual instinct must rank among the great fail-ures of history. During the nineteenth century, high noon of rationalism, the demise of religion was considered inevitable. As enlightenment spread and reactionary, church-dominated governments fell, mankind would shrug off this ancient super-stition, it was confidently predicted.

But even with atheism enshrined as the offi-cial policy of a state that exerted pervasive influ-ence over the lives of its subjects, faith survived. Consider the resources mobilized in this total warfare: mass propaganda, educational brainwash-ing, laws which forced organized religion into the catacombs, punishment for believers ranging from loss of employment to gulags. Yet with all of the weapons at its disposal, atheism was routed.

The peoples of the East clung tenaciously to their faith. Marxism was finally consumed by a flame nurtured for decades in Lutheran churches in East Germany, Catholic seminaries in Poland, and in the very shadow of the Kremlin.

It's as if the seventy-three-year horror of com-munism was no more than a divine object lesson. We were taken to the brink of the abyss and bade look in to see the fate which awaited mankind in a godless world. Humanity did an immediate about face, marching double time into the arms of that *ancient superstition*.

Give us that old time religion
(30 April 1990)

The trial of religion, first conducted by eighteenth century philosophers, is repeated in each generation. It's just the charges that keep getting sillier.

A friend clipped a news story about a fundamentalist minister who had declared war on the Easter Bunny (a pagan symbol, says he) and sent it to me with the following notation: "More proof that religion is essentially idiotic, for the intellectual coward and miserably humorless."

A typical, well-educated young American, she has been broiled and basted in skepticism by her professors, peers, and the mass media.

It's easy to focus on the more absurd proponents of any doctrine and then project this fanatical fringe as representative of the whole. Even the village atheist might scorn this line of attack as shooting Swaggarts in a barrel.

At least my correspondent didn't cite the Crusades, Inquisition, and Ayatollah in her bill of particulars. This is the other shopworn accusation against religion: its alleged responsibility for some of the bloodiest wars and oppressions in history.

It may be the easiest charge to refute. As it must be implemented by fallible creatures, any ideal can be corrupted. Dennis Prager, my favorite Jewish commentator, observes that more people have been murdered in this century in the name of

man than were killed in all previous centuries in
the name of God. The slaughterhouses of the
godless creeds span the globe. From Auschwitz
and the Katyn Forest to the Ukraine, Cambodia,
Ethiopia, and Cuba, how many have been massa-
cred in the name of self-determination, brotherhood, and compassion?

On to the indictment at hand. Religion idiotic? Is it any more rational to assume that our
marvelous minds are a biological accident, the
product of the random collision of molecules? Is
it logical to suppose that, in the final analysis, life
is futile, that after three score and seven years of
struggle and achievement we sink into oblivion?

Can it be that most of the giants of Western
history (towering intellects and believers all) were
imbeciles? The Christian apologist C.S. Lewis put
it so well when he wrote: "Really, a young atheist
cannot guard his faith too carefully. Dangers lie in
wait for him on every side."

A creed "for the intellectual coward," she says.
This is based on the assumption that the faithful
are psychologically dependent. Being of weak in-
tellect and will, they require a Big Daddy in the
sky.

In reality, the preeminent Christian and Jewish theorists were among the most rigorous thinkers. One might dispute the conclusions of a
Maimonides, an Aquinas, a Newman, or a Chesterton. But to imply that they were simple-minded,
dreaded logical analysis, bespeaks an arrogance
bred of ignorance.

Atheists may be the ultimate cowards. How
comforting it must be to believe that no matter
what one does in this existence, he is ultimately
accountable to no one, no omniscient judge will

pass on his conduct, imposing punishments for misdeeds.

"Miserably humorless?" The accusation is laughable. Lewis' *The Screwtape Letters* tickles the reader with its sardonic wit. Bishop Fulton J. Sheen, the original television theologian, had a marvelously dry sense of humor.

Woody Allen is rarely numbered among the foremost religious thinkers of our era. Yet more than any other American filmmaker, Allen deals with the eternal. His last movie, *Crimes and Misdemeanors*, was a cinematic sermon based on the irrefutable thesis that without God morality is impossible. Woody not funny? Next you'll be telling me that Groucho was a bore.

And how about those fun-loving atheists? The great unbelievers of the modern age were a dour lot. Friedrich Nietzsche, who tried to write God's obituary, was a manic depressive, a misogynist, and an intellectual precursor of fascism—a real Aryan party animal. Karl (religion-is-the-opiate-of-the-masses) Marx had a personality so poisoned that even his colleagues in the international socialist movement despised him. And Sigmund Freud, another wag. Penis envy, the Oedipus complex—what a riot.

Religion may be very bad indeed. It's just that all the secular philosophies and isms are so much worse. The indictment fails on all counts, verdict for the defendant.

What's so bad about Christian U.S.?
(8 June 1989)

The idea of America as a Christian nation has become a liberal bugaboo. But even its champions are terribly vague about their intentions.

Evan Mecham—ex-governor of Arizona who, one suspects, is tattooed with the slogan "Born to Offend"—has weighed in to the fray. Mecham, who was removed from office last year and announced his intention to seek the governorship again in 1990, is a glutton for controversy.

"Historically this is a Christian nation guaranteeing freedom to all," Mecham maintains. The governor applauds a resolution passed by the Arizona Republican Party at its convention earlier this year, which declares we are "a Christian nation based on the absolute laws of the Bible."

For secularists, those are fighting words. Harvard Law Professor Alan Dershowitz (who believes he authored the Constitution in a previous incarnation) blasts proponents of the measure as "reactionary do-badders" and "bigots (who) would (try) to turn the United States into a theocracy like the Ayatollah Khomeini's Iran." Thank heavens (it's just a figure of speech, Alan!) for dispassionate debate.

Rather than being dismissed as prejudice or simplistically hailed, the idea deserves serious consideration. Spokesmen for the Christian Right use the expression without ever defining it. Critics seem far more interested in knee-jerk condemnations and verbal over-kill than such an examination.

I think one can safely say what a "Christian

America" is not. It does not signify: the exclusion of non-Christians from public office or civic participation, the establishment of a state church, or promulgation of an official dogma.

When its devotees speak of America as a Christian nation they could mean one of the following: 1) America is Christian in the sense that an overwhelming majority of Americans are at least nominally Christian; 2) This nation was established by believing Christians, founded on Christian precepts: justice, charity, diligence, faith in divine providence; 3) America is a Christian nation today; the aforesaid values are reflected in our political/social institutions; or 4) America should be—hopefully will become—a Christian commonwealth.

Number 1 is a truism. Opinion surveys indicate that upwards of 90 percent of Americans believe in the divinity of Jesus, not that they have a clear conception of what Christianity entails, or more than a rhetorical commitment to New Testament ideals.

If #1 is self-evident, #3 is an absurdity. No one could reasonably argue that America currently is a Christian nation in terms of its essential ethos, as a glance at cable TV or the front page of your daily paper will attest. In fact, we are fast becoming an anti-Christian nation, thanks to our friends in the ACLU, People for the American Way, and the Democratic Party.

Clearly this nation was established by Christians. It was settled by men and women of devout faith. The Puritans and Pilgrims had the greatest impact on the development of our political institutions. The Declaration of Independence contains no fewer than five separate references to God, as: creator, supreme law-giver, source of rights, and "protector and patron."

As a Jew, I'm entirely comfortable with the concept of a Christian America. The morality of Christianity, though not necessarily its theology, is my morality. After all, Christians got their values from my Bible.

In a historical sense, one could speak with equal validity of America as a Jewish nation. Not that the founding fathers wore skull caps and kept kosher. (Though Cotton Mather, the great Puritan divine, did urge that Hebrew be adopted as the official language of the Massachusetts Bay Colony.) But that body of moral law which inspired our political system is based on Jewish Scriptures.

The founding fathers drew their vision of republican government (national liberty, individual rights, personal responsibility) from ancient Israel at the time of the Judges. Thomas Jefferson, who some would have us believe was an eighteenth century Norman Lear, proposed that the Great Seal of the United States depict Moses leading the children of Israel through the Red Sea, symbolizing America as the new promised land.

Our noble heritage notwithstanding, the postwar era has witnessed the triumph of secularism. Its more malignant manifestations include the legalizing of abortion, outlawing of school prayer, condoning perversion, moving toward a gender-neutral society, and public school indoctrination, beginning—but regrettably not ending—with sex education.

Should America be a Christian nation? It comes down to this: in any society, someone's

values must prevail. If America isn't animated by
the Judeo-Christian ethic it will be governed by
less enlightened doctrines. For the consequences
of the latter, check out the latest statistics on drug
use, date rape, and mental illness.

Returning Christ to Christmas
(25 December 1988)

Here's a novelty, a religious Jew who wants to
put Christ back in Christmas.

While Christmas is not my holiday, I would
like to see it celebrated in a spiritual fashion by
those who keep it. That's why I'm in favor of
public displays of religious symbols (creches and
menorahs), caroling in schools, and the like.

As a lad, I was bemused by a billboard spon-
sored by the Knights of Columbus, which urged
the public to "Keep Christ in Christmas." I considered the appeal superfluous, as I could not conceive of the holiday devoid of Jesus.

That was in the 1950s, when both America
and I were young and innocent. Today, Christmas
is increasingly observed in a secular way. At times,
that way seems overwhelming.

Seasonal television programming—from *It's a
Wonderful Life* to various versions of *A Christmas
Carol* to "A Very Brady Christmas" (gag!) and everything in between—is a paean to generosity, devotion, and other commendable conduct, without
reference to religious aspects of the yuletide.

One can wander through weeks of blinking
colored lights, plastic Santas cavorting with snow-
men on suburban lawns, kamikaze shoppers, and
red nosed-reindeer music, without ever hearing
the name of Jesus of Nazareth spoken.

For all it matters, Christmas might as well be just another national holiday, an opportunity to take time off from work, over-indulge in food and drink, and engage in a senseless orgy of gift-giving.

Yet the holiday should be a solemn, as well as a joyous, occasion. From a Christian perspective, its importance cannot be overstated, marking as it does the most direct intervention of God in human affairs—the birth of the Messiah.

The drama begun in the manger on Christmas Day wends its way through the religious calendar to a commemoration even more laden with sacred significance—Easter, and the climax of the Crucifixion and Resurrection.

This is not my theology, my way of encountering God in history. Still, I can appreciate its importance as a moral mentor for those inclined to believe. I am secure enough in my own religion not to be intimidated by the professions of faith of others who follow a different tradition. You might say I'm pro-Christmas, in a spiritual sense.

All monotheistic religions that teach ethical conduct (charity, justice, self-discipline, spirituality) are good. They inculcate virtue, the social adhesive that keeps our culture from unraveling.

Both Christianity and Judaism came into a blood-drenched pagan world and civilized it with their concept of an omnipotent God who demands righteous conduct. This is the principal reason twentieth-century paganism (Nazism and communism) despises both faiths and has labored so assiduously to eradicate them.

Ethical monotheism is the only antidote to the moral blight of our age, the only hope for a generation consumed by the worship of false gods:

sensory indulgence, relativism, utopian political creeds, and the flight from personal responsibility.

The more Christian, in the true sense of the word, America becomes, the more morally sensitive it will be and the better for all of us—Christians and non-Christians, atheists and agnostics alike.

Frankly, I'd rather live next door to a committed Christian than a secular humanist or, what's more often the case, a practicing hedonist. At least I won't have to worry about my Christian neighbor stealing my lawn mower, having wild beer bashes that spill over to the front yard, or molesting my cat.

That's why it's so important that the message of Christmas not be lost, buried under an avalanche of toys, tinsel, artificial trees, and fruit cakes. Not that I'm opposed to the festivity and merry-making, to family gatherings, feasts, and the bestowing of presents. But, at best, these are incidental to the holiday, not its substance. Frequently, they obscure the essence of Christmas.

After all, if I read the Gospels correctly, the first Christmas quite miraculously occurred in the absence of rum punch, singing chipmunks, Toys R Us, or Hallmark cards. What once was achieved surely can be duplicated.

Pope's moral message to U.S. meant for people of all faiths
(7 September 1987)

One can almost envision a band of secularist Paul Reveres galloping across the landscape, sounding the tocsin: "The pope is coming; the pope is coming!"

As P-day approaches, the media has rolled out its heavy artillery to rout the papal invasion. An NBC News special, broadcast on Aug. 25, presented a compendium of complaints from television's favorite Catholics, fussing and fretting about the Vatican's stand on abortion, homosexuality, divorce, and a host of church-related concerns.

Be sure that in days to come we will hear increasingly from the theologically disaffected with demonstrations, protestations, and fulminations by nuns who would be priests, priests who would wed, outraged abortion advocates, homosexuals who want their lifestyle validated, and feminists who demand that the pontiff amend the laws of nature to suit their purposes.

Please note, the networks never—but never—interview loyalist Catholics for these programs. Opus Dei, Bayside, and the Latin Mass folks might as well not exist as far as TV "news" coverage is concerned.

The Sept. 7 issue of *Time* magazine has a cover story titled "U.S. Catholics: A Feisty Flock Awaits the Pope" which reports, in excruciatingly minute detail over five pages, on the differences between the pope and those it chooses to designate American Catholics. The magazine breathlessly informs us that of the latter 53 percent believe priests should marry, 52 percent approve of the ordination of women, 76 percent would permit divorce and remarriage within the church, only 24 percent believe artificial birth control is wrong, and so on.

The intent, of course, is to diminish the significance of the papal sojourn, to rebut the pontiff's words, before they're even uttered, by demonstrating how many of the unfaithful are in fundamental disagreement with John Paul.

Quite frankly, I'm bored by opinion polls of pseudo-Catholics, those who attend mass twice a year, who regularly violate church doctrine, and whose trinity consists of Andrew Greeley, Phil Donahue, and Robert Drinan. Really, who cares? Religion isn't a popularity contest, neither is divine law subject to alteration by referendum. If American Catholics (hereafter, please fill in quotation marks whenever the phrase is used) can throw out moral edicts on the aforementioned, where shall the line be drawn? Adultery? Robbery? Murder?

Can you imagine where Catholicism would be today if, during the Middle Ages, church dogma had been determined by a plebiscite of the peasantry?

Picture Moses descending Mount Sinai with George Gallup at his side. Before each of the ten commandments is promulgated, the prophetic duo takes a survey to determine if it comports with the proclivities of a solid majority of the Children of Israel. ("Idolatry. All opposed? Let's see a show of hands!")

Still, the plaintive cry is heard from modernists of all stripes and denominations: "Why must John Paul be so inflexible, so intolerant of diversity . . ." cliché, cliché. The answer was eloquently provided by a traditionalist Catholic newsletter, when it recently observed: ". . . Our pilgrim Pope wills to redeem the times, not appease them."

Just so. The pope is a gentle rebuke to a godless age, as he calls us back to our spiritual roots. He is not of my faith. Nevertheless, despite doctrinal differences, all religious souls resonate to his spiritual message, his call to self-restraint, sacrifice, biblical morality, and the brotherhood of man under the fatherhood of God.

The critics and protestors are whistling past the graveyard. Their show of bravado masks a subconscious fear. His authority and humble assurance are a disturbing challenge. Lurking at the back of their minds is a nagging doubt. Possibly there is, after all, a higher law. Perhaps personal conduct should be determined not by wish or whim, but conform to the dictates of a force beyond man.

Beginning this week, John Paul II will issue his call in nine U.S. cities, over the same number of days. Those with sufficient wisdom and humility to heed his words will begin to focus not on their wants and desires, but the will of their creator. Our lords of the media—who tempt the mob with bread and "Dynasty"—should ponder that verity.

THREE

Homosexuality

The gays' advance: implacable, deadly
(24 February 1992)

The great military theorist Karl von Clausewitz wrote that victory in war lies in eliminating the enemy's will to resist. This, and nothing less, is the objective of the homosexual movement.

It seeks not mere tolerance but equality with monogamous heterosexuality, by suppressing all objections to the gay lifestyle. "Homophobia"—hatred of gays—is no longer the primary target. Now the enemy is the "heterosexist," a term of opprobrium applied to one who finds heterosexuality in any way preferable to homosexuality.

From college campuses to courtrooms to comic book pages, it's a war fought on a thousand fronts.

If New York Mayor David Dinkins has his way, when the largest St. Patrick's Day parade in the world steps down Fifth Avenue this year, a contingent from the Irish Gay and Lesbian Organization will be marching along under its own banner. His honor sicked the city's Human Rights Commission on parade organizers who oppose participation by individuals associated with virulent attacks on the Catholic church. When Cardinal O'Connor spoke at a Boston forum in January, homosexual pickets held signs condemning the prelate in scatological terms with frequent references to oral sex. And they accuse us of insensitivity.

Can there be a purer form of private conduct, of free expression, than a parade? But any manifestation of opposition to our newest minority must be rooted out.

When *Peninsula*, a conservative magazine at Harvard, had the impudence to publish an issue dispassionately analyzing the controversy, making the ethical case against gay sex without acrimony or invective, homosexual groups put up posters with the names and dorm numbers of *Peninsula* editors, inviting harassment calls at hours most likely to disturb sleep.

Our leading centers of open inquiry are closed to dissent from erotic orthodoxy. Over one hundred colleges and universities have codes that bar discrimination based on "sexual orientation."

Words that homosexuals find offensive can bring a firing-squad response. No similar effort is made to protect the sensibilities of heterosexuals. Students at Rutgers report cruising in the library's basement bathroom, with males exposing their genitals, a perversion the administration tacitly condones. Says Jason T. Brown, president of the Rutgers College student government: "The university totally caves in to any demand the gays make."

On the judicial front, advances continue. Several weeks after California Governor Pete Wilson vetoed a gay rights law, in response to an outpouring of public opposition, its substance was judicially-legislated by the California State Court of Appeals. Two weeks ago, a Texas district court overturned a ban on homosexuals in the Dallas police force. What militants can't wring out of craven politicians, compliant judges hand them on a silver platter.

Late last month, a Manhattan surrogate court judge approved the adoption of a six-year-old boy by his mother's lesbian lover. The court claimed it could discern no disadvantage to the child from being raised in such an environment. The omniscient jurist somehow overlooked a recent study in the *Journal of Sex Research* indicating that "31 percent of lesbians . . . reported being victims of forced sex by their current or most recent partner," with battery frequently employed.

And in March, Marvel Comics introduced the first gay super-hero who battles homophobia and AIDS discrimination. (Whatever happened to truth, justice, and the American way?) "And who, disguised as a mild-mannered dancer for a great metropolitan ballet company . . ."

Though the odds are increasingly desperate— family advocates are like the French army of 1940, systematically outflanked, enveloped, overrun— surrender is unthinkable.

If homosexuality is legitimized, no perversion (sadomasochism, incest, sex with children) can logically be opposed.

A healthy society is life-affirming. Homosexuality is the metaphysical negation of life. Incapable of reproduction (giving life), it can replenish its numbers only by seduction. Many of the sex acts preferred by homosexuals involve pain, degradation, or a combination of the two—conducive to neither physical nor psychological well-being, one reason there are such high percentages of mental disorders and sexually-transmitted diseases among homosexuals.

To surrender on this issue would be a capitulation of the entire Judeo-Christian ethic.

Judaism and gays: A faith divided
(26 July 1990)

Barney Frank and his lifestyle are the subject of considerable debate in Jewish circles. One commentator delineates the unbridgeable chasm which separates the Jewish ethic from the homoerotic culture.

While the National Association of Reform Rabbis has determined to ordain homosexuals, an Orthodox rabbinic court announced it had excommunicated the gay Massachusetts congressman for "desecrating the name of God and the Jewish people."

Orthodox Judaism bases its stand on the biblical injunction against homosexuality. Reform counters that the Jewish faith has always stressed tolerance and compassion.

Into the fray steps Dennis Prager—author, lecturer, and probably the most perceptive Jewish thinker in America today. Yeshiva-educated, Prager is the co-author of two highly acclaimed books about Judaism and gives more than two hundred lectures a year to largely Jewish audiences. In the latest installment of his Los Angeles-based newsletter, "Ultimate Issues," he confronts the controversy head on.

Prager begins by noting that Judaism alone among religions of the ancient world opposed homosexuality. In Greece and Rome, among the Phoenicians and Canaanites, a man's preference for other men, or boys, was of no more consequence than another's choice of beef over mutton.

Judaism was the first religion to insist that sex be confined to marital relations. The Torah excoriates homosexual acts, calling them an "abomination," a term reserved for the gravest offenses: idolatry, human sacrifice, and ritual prostitution. The Torah warned Jews that if they followed the customs of the Canaanites, sodomy among them, the holy land they were about to inherit would "vomit them out."

Prager observes that Judaism started a moral revolution, later carried forward by Christianity, in demanding that sex be sanctified, raised from an animal to a spiritual plane. By sublimating man's "polymorphous sex drive," Judeo-Christian ethics made civilization possible.

By insisting that romantic love could be found only in marriage, it began the process of raising the status of woman from breeding animal to fully human. It's no coincidence that in those societies where homosexuality was and is widespread (ancient Greece, the Arab world today) "women were relegated to society's periphery."

While he believes that homosexuals deserve understanding, Prager firmly opposes the central idea of the gay rights movement: social sanction for homosexuality.

"It is impossible for Judaism to make peace with homosexuality," Prager writes, "because homosexuality denies many of Judaism's most fundamental values. It denies life; it denies God's express desire that men and women cohabit; and it denies the root structure of Judaism's wish for all mankind, the family."

Remember the old joke: God created Adam and Eve, not Adam and Steve. No kidding, says Prager. As His reason for forming Eve, the Bible explains: "It is not good for man to be alone." Adds Prager: "Now, presumably, in order to solve the problem of man's aloneness, God could have created another man, or even a community of men. . . . Man's solitude was not a function of his not being with other people; it was a function of his being without a woman."

Judaism, says Prager, worries about the social consequences of men without women—the unrestrained sexuality, the violence, the live-for-the-moment ethos. Unlike other religions, far from esteeming celibacy, Judaism holds it a sin. In ancient Israel, an unmarried man could not become the high priest. A man without children couldn't serve on the supreme religious tribunal—all a testament to Judaism's belief in the humanizing qualities of marriage and families.

"The union of male and female is not merely some lovely ideal; it is the essence of the Jewish outlook on becoming human. To deny it is tantamount to denying a primary purpose of life." Prager observes.

To the claim that homosexuals are simply following their nature, Prager responds that the preponderance of evidence contradicts this. Even if it is true that certain individuals are thus inclined, so what? Doubtless, some are inclined to adultery, seeking sex with children and other perversions. As the chief rabbi of the United Kingdom explained in his paper on AIDS, the bedrock of Jewish moral teaching is on man transcending his nature.

In those societies where homosexuality was condoned (such as Athens, which idealized masculine nudity and wrote homoerotic poetry), the practice flourished. Prager warns: "A society's values, much more than individual tendencies, determine the extent of homosexuality in that society." Hence the peril of gay rights laws, legal sanction for gay marriage, and presenting homosexuality as an alternative lifestyle in school curriculum.

Prager ends with a call for Judaism to return to its historic mission. That America's elite believes all forms of sexual behavior are equally valid should matter no more than the moral judgments of the ancient Greeks and Romans. "It is the task of Judaism to be a light unto the nations, not to follow the nations' darkness," Prager declares. Did I say he was one of the most discerning Jewish thinkers? He's also one of the most courageous.

FOUR

New Age/Humanism/Paganism

Beware of the real humanist agenda
(9 June 1988)

In the past presidential election, the very existence of secular humanism was hotly contested. It was, we were assured, a bugaboo—a term concocted by fundamentalist preachers, tripping on apple pie, to sway their credulous flocks.

For a fictitious philosophy *sans* adherents, the creed appears to be thriving. On April 24, an organization called the American Humanist Association placed a large display ad in that premier organ of establishment wisdom—the *New York Times*.

"What On Earth is Humanism?" the solicitation rhetorically inquires. "A Joyous Life Affirming Philosophy That Relies On (a flourish of trumpets would be nice here) Reason, Science And Democracy"—the trinity of our secular society. Sounds like a promotion for an underarm deodorant: Convenient, goes on dry, and helps stop wetness three ways.

Humanism, the ad advises, abjures faith in God and "believes in an ethic of morality that grounds all human values in this earthly experiences and relationships and holds as its greatest goal the happiness, freedom and progress of all humanity in this one and only life."

The non-theistic theology has a venerable lineage. "Humanism was initiated by the ancient Greeks, such as Aristotle . . . incorporates in its synthesis the sound elements of other philosophies, including the naturalistic viewpoints of John Dewey, George Santayana and Bertrand Russell."

Now we're getting somewhere. Russell was a hoary apologist for Soviet repression, Dewey (a founding member of the American Humanist Association and signer of the 1933 Humanist Manifesto I) is the father of progressive, read permissive, education.

What children learn is irrelevant, it's how they're conditioned for the coming new order that's important, Dewey held. Public schools which produce functional illiterates, while socializing students via sex education and peace studies, are a testimony to his influence over the institution.

"There may be humanists all around you," the ad exults. Indeed. The signers of the Humanist Manifesto II (1973) include Alan Guttmacher, past president of Planned Parenthood; Betty Friedan, founder of the National Organization for Women; and environmental determinism guru B.F. Skinner.

Humanism has spawned the melange of movements which dominate and direct the social policy debate: feminism, population control/abortion, gay rights, a crusading secularism, and the see-no-evil disarmament movement.

The legions of humanism include Hollywood screenwriters selling relativism and hedonism, social scientists who deny individual responsibility, hemophiliac jurists, advocates of one-world/collectivist government, and prelates who substitute social activism for Scriptures.

But the Humanist Association is far too modest in its historical name-dropping. Other forerunners of the ism include French philosopher Jean Jacques Rousseau (intellectual progenitor of the Reign of Terror) and Karl Marx. Said the latter, "Humanism is the denial of God and the total affirmation of man. . . . (as such) Humanism is nothing else but Marxism."

While spurning God, the Humanist Association attempts to cleverly cash in on popular regard for the Judeo-Christian ethic. Thus the ad avows that humanism "embodies the ethical ideals of various religions, especially Christianity. . . . Jesus in the New Testament gave voice to such Humanistic hopes as social equality, human brotherhood and peace on earth."

Wrong. Very wrong. In fact, humanism and monotheism are metaphysical galaxies apart. The former espouses situational ethics (a morality of convenience) the latter ethical absolutism. Like Rousseau, humanists believe man, resplendent in his natural goodness, is corrupted by society. Christians and Jews believe in sin, the failings of the heart.

The monotheistic faiths teach free will and personal accountability. Humanists deny the existence of one and thus the applicability of the other.

Without God, morality is impossible. Right and wrong become matters of personal preference. You think murder is wrong; I don't. It's your opinion against mine. In the Decalogue, Thou-shalt-not-kill is followed by the declaration

"I am the Lord your God." The commandment's force comes from its source.

Reason, democracy, science? All fine within their realm, but none an adequate substitute for transcendental values. Each can be corrupted.

Reason has been employed to justify the most monstrous evils. The German philosophers (Nietzche, Hegel) provided the rationale for Nazism. Adolf Hitler came to power through the democratic process. The German scientists were devoted servants of the state, willing suppliers of the technology for Auschwitz.

Humanists are all around us, many blissfully unaware of the ideology they've embraced. Humanism is the dominant ethos of our culture, a deadly, deterministic creed which seeks to set up mankind as an idol, upon the desecrated altar of God. Hosannas are offered to the secular trinity, but totalitarians will be the ultimate beneficiaries of the service.

Earth movement finds pagan roots
(22 April 1992)

Be sure to bring an amulet, incense, and perhaps a crystal to this year's Earth Day extravaganza. The ecology movement has gotten back to its pagan roots.

Reporting on Earth Day, 1991, *Time* magazine informed its readers: "Nature worship was part of . . . (the) festivities from Boston . . . to Berkeley . . . The ceremonies were part of the growing U.S. spiritual movement: Goddess worship, the effort to create a female-centered focus for spiritual expression."

The cultural establishment is exceedingly tolerant of this idolatrous fad. "But if it (eco-religion) appears flaky on the surface, it still warrants sympathy and respect. For it proceeds from values of nurturing, peace and harmony with nature," the *New York Times* editorialized on 12 May 1991.

A Sierra Club handbook ("Well Body, Well Earth") offers Buddhist meditation and Hopi rituals as a way to "reaffirm our bonds with the *spirit of the living earth.*" Children are initiated into the mystery cult via the popular Saturday morning cartoon "Captain Planet," a product of Turner Network Television. Ted Turner (who once called Christianity a religion for "losers") is a classic tree-hugger whose Better World Society promulgates an environmentalist creed to replace the Ten Commandments. ("I promise to have love and respect for Planet Earth.")

In the series, the Earth Goddess Gaia awakens to fight polluters. She chooses five children from around the world as her surrogates. Armed with magic rings that harness the power of the earth, water, wind, and fire, they are sent forth to battle oil companies and other corporate heretics. Letting your kids watch this stuff is like turning them over to a Druid priest for religious education.

The mainline Protestant churches all have been infected. At its biennial convention in Canberra, Australia, last year, the World Council of Churches proclaimed: "Those who are closest to the land and whose spiritualities *consider the earth to be sacred,* are those best able to guide this new process (environmental renewal)."

The increasingly popular dogma is—like so much of environmentalism—based on myth: that in the beginning people existed harmoniously with nature (actually, they lived in stark terror of it), in peaceful societies which worshipped the Mother Goddess. This utopia was destroyed by patriarchal religions (Judaism and Christianity) with their progressive outlook and obedience to a deity beyond nature who gave humanity command of the material world.

Environmental pagans view Judeo-Christian faith as the source of ecological evil, from oil spills to global warming. "We shall continue to have a worsening ecologic crisis until we reject the Christian axiom that nature has no reason for existence save to serve man," writes environmental theorist Lynn White, Jr.

But if Genesis is correct (1:26, "Let us make man . . . and let them have domination . . . over all the earth . . ."), that is exactly why the physical world was created, for the benefit of mankind. In the pagan cosmology, nature—eternal, omnipotent—is the deity, that which is to be worshipped. In the Judeo-Christian worldview, God is above nature, having created it *ex nihilo*.

The god of ecology is impersonal, cold to the point of brutal indifference. There is no appeal from its judgement. (Anyone who thinks nature is benevolent should watch a lion devouring its prey live.) Nature doesn't heal the sickly child, but—on the principle of survival of the fittest—ordains that it die. The next time a family member is ill, try praying to a ponderosa pine.

The idyllic picture neo-pagans paint of monotheism's precursors never existed. In reality, paganism was as cruel and bloody as that which it hallowed. Instead of sacrificing trees for men, men (though more often women) were literally sacrificed for nature—to ensure that the rains came in their proper season and the crops grew.

Traditional religion has always held the doctrine of stewardship, that man has the authority to use nature wisely, not to squeeze every last drop out of it, but to cultivate it, preserving the rich heritage for future generations.

It was nineteenth century veneration of man and his industrial achievements ("Glory to man in the highest. The maker and master of things," wrote the poet Algernon Charles Swinburne)—of Promethean man freed from religious constraints—that led to the devaluing of nature, rape of the land, and the pollution crisis.

Now ecologists would push the pendulum too far in the opposite direction, not by respecting, but by revering nature. As their spiritual forerunners did, ecologists are dragging humans off to the sacrificial altar. In the coming ecological Eden, people will toil, surrendering the greater portion of their income for the rain forest, the ozone layer, and other trendy idols.

Witchcraft declared a religion
(12 June 1989)

Should the United States government recognize witchcraft as a religion? The question is fast becoming moot.

Item: An Air Force woman who says she's a witch has been granted time off to celebrate her "religious holidays," including All Hallow's Eve. Airman Patricia Hutchins (a self-proclaimed disciple of "wiccan") was supported in her request by the chaplain at her base in San Antonio, Texas.

Item: The U.S. District Court for the Southern District of Mississippi ruled that Jamie Dodge's dismissal from employment with the Salvation Army constituted unlawful discrimination. Dodge was fired after a supervisor caught her using the office photocopier to reproduce material relating to what was characterized as a "satanic ritual."

The court held that since the Salvation Army was the recipient of federal funding for the project on which Dodge was working, it could not discriminate on the basis of religion.

Take the foregoing to their logical conclusions. Will we soon see Druid chaplains in the armed forces, giant flashing pentagrams as part of Halloween displays in public parks, tax exemptions for sacred groves, a witch stamp issued by the postal service (from Salem, of course)?

Modern witchcraft (support your local coven) is an integral part of the New Age movement, which is spreading like a social disease. There are over 2,500 New Age bookstores nationwide. Nearly every record store has a section for New Age music.

Fortune 500 corporations are buying in with human-potential seminars. The Aquarian philosophy is propagated by a host of catalogue services hawking audio and video cassettes, which promise health, wealth, and wisdom to those whose nativity (every sixty seconds) P.T. Barnum immortalized. Shirley MacLaine, star of the new "spiritual workout" video, is the sect's most visible shaman.

There is a real danger in government sanctioning this mumbo-jumbo creed. Religion warrants official recognition and support, as our founding fathers understood. The New Age cult might more accurately be described as an anti-religion. True faith brings us closer to God; New Age paganism takes us further from Him.

Consider the pillars of New Age enlightenment (witchcraft, call it what you will):

Pantheism—an impersonal deity. While Western religion posits one God, omnipotent and actively involved with his creation, the New Age offers a multiplicity of deities—all passive, offering neither hope nor help to mankind.

Nature is God. The principal deity is nature itself; its various manifestations are aspects of the godhead. This has considerable appeal for Sixties nature freaks who despise industrial society and seek virtue in pristine field and forest—naiveté based on a total ignorance of the random cruelty of nature.

Man is God. As a part of nature (rather than a being separate and apart from the natural world, as Judaism and Christianity postulates), man himself is a deity, or is capable of becoming divine by getting in touch with his essence (by contemplating his navel while listening to sitar music, or scaling a mountain to chant for world peace).

Morality is relative. Since man is divine, he becomes his own law-giver. This is a prescription for moral anarchy and unbridled hedonism. Released from the *oppressive* strictures of monotheistic faith, values are based on intuition, whim, or the teachings of some moth-eaten guru.

Man creates his own reality. If man is God, it stands to reason that, like God, he can shape reality—hence modern witchcraft, sympathetic magic, "Mystic crystal revelations and the mind's true liberation."

This is the perfect dogma for late twentieth century society. It offers salvation of sorts (reincarnation, merging with the cosmic consciousness) without more effort than suspension of the critical faculty, certainly without the need for moral discipline. It may be appealing to burned-out hippies and rootless yuppies, but religion it is not.

As far as I'm concerned, Shirley MacLaine can fondle her crystals till her hands grow numb, and modern witches dance by the light of the silvery moon till they drop from exhaustion. But for the federal government to sanction this pantheistic prattle is blasphemous.

Like Rome in the declining years of the empire, barbarians are at the gates. Government, which should be holding the fort, instead is lifting the portcullis to admit them.

Rights activists turn to jungle law
(1 January 1989)

It had to happen eventually: Animal-rights activists have become completely unhinged.

• A group called the Animal Liberation Front has claimed responsibility for the pre-Christmas fire bombing of four department stores in the United Kingdom, to protest the sale of fur coats. No one was injured, but one business was gutted in the ensuing conflagration.

• In early November, police arrested Fran Stephanie Trutt, a substitute teacher from Queens. Trutt, a decorated member of the Legion of Lassie, is charged with planting a pipe bomb studded with roofing nails outside the headquarters of U.S. Surgical Corp., which uses dogs to train doctors in the use of its high-speed surgical staplers.

• After an eighteen-month protest by a group called Trans-Species Unlimited, the Cornell Medical School has agreed to abandon a fourteen-year project using cats to study the effects of barbiturates. This marks the first time animal activists have derailed important research work.

• In July, Sweden (the home of really weird social experiments) enacted a bill of rights for farm animals. Henceforth, pigs must be granted separate bedding and feeding places, cattle will have grazing rights, and chickens must be given freedom of the barnyard. Astrid Lindgren, the measure's principal proponent, is opposed to artificial insemination and would like to see cows granted conjugal visits by bulls.

Kooky? Dangerous? You bet, and also the logical culmination of the animal-rights movement. There was a time when old ladies in tennis shoes (of all ages and both sexes) confined their dementia to marching in anti-vivisection protests. Now they are vandalizing laboratories, harassing researchers, and invading the political arena.

I suppose I have to say it: I am very much opposed to unnecessary cruelty to animals (please note the qualifier). I've had pets most of my life. My family shares its domicile with a cat and a dog. My religion stresses kindness to animals. Jewish law was the first to require the humane treatment of the same. To be kosher, those raised for food have to be slaughtered in the least painful manner. On the Sabbath, even work animals must be allowed to rest.

But Judaism also recognizes the clear distinction between man and beast. It is this differentiation that the Bambi Brigade seeks to obliterate. The blurring of distinctions—between men and women, adults and children, the normal and abnormal, and people and animals—is part of the intellectual sloppiness of our age.

It's also a consequence of society's slide to modern paganism. Without a God in whose spiritual image man was created, humans become just another grouping in the Wild Kingdom. Raising animals to the level of man lowers man to the status of animals.

This is the philosophical thrust of the animal-rights movement—that man is no better than other creatures. Hence, denizens of field and forest must be afforded the same treatment and dignity as humanity.

Animal advocates even have a designation for denial of this premise; they call it "speciesism" (the bigoted notion that human beings are superior to Larry the lab rat), a term intended to damn the attitude as an evil commensurate with racism and other forms of vile discrimination.

Be clear on this: Their goal isn't to shelter animals from abuse, but to elevate them. When the movement's chief theoretician postulates that whales have a right to privacy, which is violated by whale-watching cruises, that is far removed from the noble work of the ASPCA. When animal advocates protested the transplantation of a baboon's heart into an infant several years ago (on the grounds that we have no right to sacrifice one "life form" for another), it was the clearest possible indication of the movement's mindset.

The buddies of beasts know full well that humans benefit immensely from animal experimentation. Many miracle drugs would not be on the market today absent such research. Surgeons could not be trained in the application of lifesaving procedures without using laboratory dogs.

Animal advocates have made a conscious choice to sacrifice people for pets. That they would

turn to the law of the jungle to protect furry crit-
ters is utterly predictable.

FIVE

Morality/Sexuality

From 'making love' to 'having sex': intimacy is dying
(22 July 1991)

The trouble with the Demi Moore maternity-ward centerfold on the cover of *Vanity Fair* isn't that it's pornographic. Anyone who's aroused by the sight of a naked woman eight months pregnant—who looks like she swallowed Peru—is beyond perversion. Indecent it's not; unseemly it is.

No, Ms. Moore's novel exhibitionism in hot pursuit of publicity and the magazine's circulation pandering are symptoms of a problem more than skin-deep: the near extinction of privacy. If our society has a credo it's this: everything must be discussed, displayed, demonstrated.

Pregnancy should be an intensely private time. The life germinating within quite naturally occasions introspection, reflection, a desire to be alone to contemplate a miracle in the making. That's why the sight of a pregnant woman exhibiting herself in the raw to millions of magazine readers is so disquieting.

There is a war on modesty, the magnitude of which makes Operation Desert Storm seem like a

Boy Scout encampment. We salivate for details of
the private lives of famous people. A just-pub-
lished book on the extramarital romps of JFK is
destined for best-seller status.

Talk-show hosts incite guests to explicitness.
Interviewed on the "Arsenio Hall Show" recently,
Ali MacGraw claimed she once posed nude for a
famous painter. According to the actress, at one
point the elderly artist crawled under a table and
began licking her toes. Only a cynic would assume
the revelation was related to the fact that MacGraw
is a has-been who by her embarrassing assertion
sought to assure a return engagement on the program.

The disorder isn't limited to the Beverly Hills
booboisie. On almost any public beach you'll see
women sashaying around in thong-bikinis that
would make Madonna (justify her lust) blanch.
Heavily advertised telephone hotlines allow callers to share the most intimate details of their
private lives with total strangers or drool over the
confessions of others.

A Boston radio talk show host saw his ratings
soar when he conducted an on-air, no-holds-barred
sex survey for women. Callers fought for the opportunity to do a psychic striptease by describing
their favorite locations for intercourse (answers
included against a chain-link fence and on top of
a washing machine), preferred positions, homosexual encounters, date they lost their virginity,
etc.—in an orgy of indiscretion which might be
mistaken for a Kinsey Institute telethon.

As a result of this exhibitionism/voyeurism
saturation, our culture is increasingly detached
and dehumanized. We'd rather rent X-rated vid-

eos than be intimate. People talk about "having sex" (an appropriately mechanical term), where formerly they spoke of "making love."

The most commonly voiced complaint among young couples is the inability to be intimate, the paucity of sexual encounters combined with emotional connection, or the lack of sex, period.

Rabbi Manis Friedman titled his recently published book *Doesn't Anyone Blush Anymore?* The rabbi argues that intimacy problems are a direct result of a lack of privacy. That, even in marriage, people need their space. That the pressure to be open about our bodies and how we misuse them leads to anxiety which stifles the sex drive.

"Intimacy is sharing something with only one person," the rabbi asserts. "If it's shared indiscriminately, it loses its sanctity." Of the Moore photograph, he observes: "That's one more part of her life she'll never be able to call her own. Because she's shared it with the public, she's lost it. Her self is diminished."

The soul is calloused. In New York City last week, dozens of motorists stopped to gawk, but made no move to intervene, while a man allegedly raped his three-year-old niece. Perhaps they thought they were watching a movie or viewing a magazine cover. The term "decency" has an ethical as well as a sexual connotation.

People have appetites which often are quite ugly. Society's business, through law and custom, is to hold those natural but unpleasant urges in check, so that we may be truly human, instead of animals which walk on their hind legs.

There's a Talmudic saying that however debased a man, if he retains the capacity to blush (if he feels shame), he isn't beyond redemption. Increasingly, our society is losing that ability. We've sold our patrimony (the opportunity for holiness) for glossy stock, videotape, late-night, long-distance dross. Moore is helping to shape the world her unborn child will inherit, a form of abuse far worse than bruises and cigarette burns.

Whose morality matters?
(3 June 1991)

How fortunate we are to live in an age in which moral instruction is both plentiful and accessible. Our liberal friends are always on hand to teach us virtue.

A letter from a reader, composed between violent knee spasms, complaining about a piece I wrote on sexual ethics, made me painfully aware of my own shortcomings in this regard and anxious to remedy the situation. "I recently read yet another of your heartless, narrow-minded articles," the letter from Martin begins. He somehow overlooked "insensitive" and "mean-spirited," choice invectives from the liberal lexicon.

"I really need to ask you a question," my correspondent continued. "Who has made you God? What makes your morality better than other people's morality?" After a few paragraphs of unsolicited psychoanalysis, he closes with: "Compassion and tolerance is (sic) something you need to work on."

What makes my morality better than other people's morality? As the king said in *Amadeus*, "Well, there it is"—moral relativism. The question implies far more than my inquisitor comprehends.

Whether or not he realizes it, the writer is also asking: What makes the Judeo-Christian ethic superior to modern paganism? What makes the volunteer at a drug rehab center better than a schoolyard pusher? What makes someone who runs a shelter for battered women better than a wife-beater? What makes the morality of those who hid Jews during the Holocaust superior to those who killed them?

But we all know that genocide, family violence, and the Colombian version of better-living-through-chemistry are wrong. Or do we? The rejection of each is based on one of those parochial moral judgments. If morality is subjective, who's to say one choice is preferable to another? Every vice and depravity to which humanity is heir has its intellectual champions. If you doubt this, read the Marquis de Sade, a leftist thinker who argued passionately for sexual brutality.

What makes my morality better? Well, Martin, old buddy, old pal, when my repressive, Victorian values were in vogue, we didn't have one million teen-age pregnancies annually, 60 percent of black children born out-of-wedlock, a third of married respondents to a survey confessing they commit adultery, and half of all girls between fifteen and nineteen sexually active.

We didn't have twenty thousand homicides a year, multi-generational welfare families, or one out of two marriages ending in divorce. A 62 percent increase in the rate of teen-age syphilis in a two-year period and half of all high school seniors reporting they've used illicit drugs were beyond our wildest imaginings. As a visit to any prison, morgue, or VD clinic will attest, moral choices have consequences.

But, perhaps I'm wrong. They say everyone has something to teach us, and liberals constantly hold themselves up as models of rectitude. To whom among them should I turn for instruction in compassion?

Perhaps the esteemed U.S. Senator Edward Moore Kennedy, the party boy with a selective hearing impediment (deafness to the cries of women in distress)—who, when questioned about an alleged rape at his family's Palm Beach estate, suddenly became Sgt. Schultz from "Hogan's Heroes" ("I know noss-ing!")—could give me a crash course in caring.

I'm eager for instruction in decency from the AIDS activists who disrupt church services and throw condoms at priests. Surely the affirmative action crowd (editorial writers, college administrators, politicians), comfortable, middle-class professionals who would sacrifice the educational opportunities and careers of others to assuage their conscience—confident that their own lives will never be used to balance the scales of social justice—can enlighten me on the quality of mercy. The humanitarians who shed copious tears for welfare recipients, but have trouble mustering much sympathy for tax serfs, have cornered the market on benevolence.

I'm sure I could learn a lot about tolerance from the P.C. bully boys who roam our college campuses, assaulting speakers, shouting down those who dissent from their dogma. Hollywood—which regularly reviles priests as fornicators, ministers as larcenous lechers, and devout Christians as superstitious bigots—can further sensitize me.

There's so much to learn from the paragons

of the left. Surely they can help to heal my heart-less ways. I only fear there may not be time enough in one life to absorb all of their invaluable lessons.

Sex addicts: Newest victims
(18 June 1990)

"Stop me before I fornicate again." That's the anguished cry of the newest "my-body-chemis-try-made-me-do-it" victim group—sex addicts.

Recently, three hundred sex educators and researchers met in Minneapolis, mecca of reflex liberalism, to excavate the roots of the phenom-enon. The star of the conference was Patrick Carnes, a therapist and author of *Out of the Shad-ows: Understanding Sexual Addiction*.

Carnes describes the newly minted ailment as "a loss of control and willingness to risk any kind of consequence for a pleasure that gets you so hooked you can not stop." Pop psychology meets the *Playboy* philosophy.

Organizations like Sex and Love Addicts Anonymous, Sexual Compulsives Anonymous, and Sexaholics Anonymous (all modeled after A.A.) claim twenty thousand members nationally. Ac-cording to a 1987 *Time Magazine* article, meetings feature such comic confessions as "My name is Joe, and I'm a sex addict" or one participant's daffy declaration that he is an "orgasm addict."

Is there any form of human behavior not now explicable in terms of irresistible impulse? Cancer-stricken smokers and their families regu-larly sue tobacco companies on the theory that once R.J. Reynolds had them hooked, they were the slaves of nicotine. Child abuse? The abuser

himself was a childhood victim. Rapists are acting
out of rage beyond their control. Sin has become
abnormality. Therapy takes the place of repentance.

Even in our licentious age, people still feel
the nagging tug of conscience. In order to assuage
our guilt, we needs must pretend that the fault
lies not in ourselves but in chromosomes and
hormones.

The man cheating on his wife is the pawn of
biological destiny. The woman intimately acquainted with the Sixth Fleet suffers from a crav-
ing which—absent professional help—cannot be
denied.

Only a Ph.D. would be loony enough to fall
for this fraud. Promiscuity is the easiest thing in
the world to understand. As French writer Henri
de Montherlant put it, promiscuity "is not just
man's most natural instinct, it is also his most
reasonable instinct. I have picked an apple, I found
it good. I want another: nothing more reasonable
than to pick that too."

It's no accident that the sex act is among the
most delightful of human experiences. He who
gave us our nature intended it so. He wants us to
be happy. Moreover, He made the act pleasurable
to prompt us to achieve His purpose: marriage
and the creation of families, procreation, and the
nurturing of successive generations. In the joy of
the sex act does humanity find its future.

But, like every other pleasure (food, fun, pros-
perity), sexual ecstasy is a double-edged sword.
What gives us intense pleasure can also be the
source of mortification. Those who surrender to
their appetites in the end are consumed by them.

What experience compares with the wretchedness of the post-coital realization that one has shared physical intimacy with a stranger, has had intercourse not with a person (one whom we know in the deepest sense, and who knows us in turn), but with a body, that we have used and been used in the most sordid fashion? As the female protagonist in a recent film devastatingly inquired of her Don Juanish counterpart: "Have you ever made love to a woman who was your friend?"

The origin of the problem is the effort to divorce sexuality from spirituality, to treat sex as a drive, instead of a divine gift. If a gift, then it should be properly appreciated, used as the giver ordained. In his classic work *Orthodoxy*, G.K. Chesterton stated: "We should thank God for beer and burgundy by not drinking too much of them."

By curbing our sexual appetites, we show proper gratitude for this wonderful benefaction. By using the gift as intended, we realize its fullest potential. By misusing it, we transform it from a blessing to a curse. Little wonder "sex addicts" describe each conquest as a hollow experience.

Sex addicts could save themselves a bundle on therapy, and embarrassing evenings of public confessions, by learning the lesson of Ecclesiastes: the single-minded pursuit of pleasure (divorced from charity, duty, or gratitude) leads to the dead end of dissolution.

Our pursuit of the perfect body
(28 January 1990)

You just can't escape them. The health and beauty-mongers are everywhere, insistently urging us to shape up, shed pounds, smooth out, become the new, beautiful us we were always meant to be.

Listening to the radio, I was accosted by a commercial for (ugh!) male liposuction. Come to a free seminar, I was implored. Meet satisfied customers. Learn how to rid myself of love-handles, double chins, protuberant bellies, and the like.

I fled the aesthetic assault by turning to a magazine, only to be ambushed by an ad offering "clear, smooth, younger-looking skin—guaranteed," with the miracle Peelaway Process wrinkle remover. This was illustrated with before and after shots, one showing a wrinkled old woman, next to a photo of the same lady (looking every bit as ancient) *sans* wrinkles.

Let's not be too hard on American enterprise, which, after all, doesn't create the demand, but merely panders to it. Americans are avid in their pursuit of physical beauty and rejuvenation. We could feed a medium-sized Third World nation for eternity on what we annually spend on cosmetics and hair coloring alone.

It seems that half of the country is constantly dieting. Some programs, providing prepackaged grub, dole out calories like a miser spending his pocket change. Others stage events that are combination revival meetings/Chinese brainwashing sessions.

But dieting alone isn't enough. Oh, no; we must firm up, shape up, tone up those flaccid muscles. From Richard Simmons, to the boom industry of health clubs, to home-exercise equipment, I smell America sweating, doggedly pumping the pedals of Lifecycle machines in pursuit of the elusive physical ideal.

There's nothing intrinsically wrong with moderate concern about one's appearance. And, yes, valid health considerations often incline us to diet and exercise. But the current passion for face and figure are, to say the least, obsessive.

The origins of this fixation aren't difficult to discern. The media constantly bombard us with sleek, sinuous, curvaceous, or well-muscled images of corporeal perfection.

Movies that a generation ago presented seductive physiques at least minimally attired today offer hard bodies in all of their fleshy splendor. Breasts defy gravity, abdomens are as flat as a Kansas landscape, tight little bottoms sway alluringly. Advertising does its part. An ad for Nivea skin cream—of a nude model, head thrown back, an expression of ecstasy on her face—formerly would have been banned in Boston.

The unadulterated skin magazines play second fiddle to the amateurs. Still, they permit men to crave the *au naturel* images of women they could never hope to possess in real life, who—come to think of it—probably don't exist outside the airbrushed pages of *Playboy* and *Penthouse*.

It is all so terribly futile. Time is the ultimate equalizer. Ingrid Bergman possibly was the most beautiful woman who ever drew breath, a veritable goddess in *Spellbound*. At the end, the ravages of age had taken their ghastly toll on her face and form. Cold creams, Grecian Formula, Nautilus, face-lifts, tummy tucks, and liposuction all are raw recruits thrown in the path of an unstoppable foe.

Still, we eagerly pursue the unattainable. Our lives have become so hectic and brutal that all that seems to matter is the ephemeral—the tantalizing sight, the rapturous moment. Out with the old and the ugly, in with the young and yummy. If it doesn't look good, switch the channel, flip the page, divorce the middle-aged Mrs., marry the comely coed.

Have we become so hollow that we can only perceive that which confronts the eyes? Have we lost the ability to see with our hearts, to detect beauty in a lined face, in a less than perfect complexion, in a plump figure, in a form which deviates in the least from the Adonis/Aphrodite ideal?

If only we cared for inner beauty the way we agonize over loose skin and a little middle-age spread. If we devoted half the time and attention to the health of our spirits that we lavish on this physical form we possess for a fleeting moment of eternity, perhaps we could achieve the temporal glory of a world without liposuction ads.

Our lyin', cheatin' hearts will do us in
(16 May 1991)

The crisis of our age may be summed up in the computer programmer's acronym: GIGO—garbage in, garbage out. Or, in the words of Professor Richard M. Weaver, ideas have consequences.

We cannot constantly pump people's psyches with raw sewage and expect the end product to smell like springtime in the Rockies. A new study, which serves as the basis for a forthcoming book, *The Day America Told the Truth*, should set alarm bells clanging in our national consciousness.

The poll plumbs the depths of our lyin', cheatin' hearts. According to the survey, 70 percent of Americans have no heroes. Only 13 percent believe in all Ten Commandments. The least popular precept may be judged by the disclosure that a third of married men and women confess to at least one extramarital relationship.

But the cheatin' isn't confined to affairs of the heart. Over 90 percent admit to lying regularly, at home and at work. Close to a majority call in sick when they're not. Most workers claim they waste seven hours a week. Oh, and—hide the cyanide—7 percent would commit murder for $2 million.

This ethos has been a long time in the making. Churches, schools, government, and media all have done a fine job of cultivating immorality in the name of compassion.

The Presbyterian Church (USA) is to debate an historic document which, says *Newsweek*, "reads like a sermon on Eros prepared in the heat of politically correct passion."

"Keeping Body and Soul Together" urges a thorough revision of church teaching on sexual mores, a Gospel of St. Madonna. Out with "patriarchalism," "heterosexist" assumptions, and passing moral judgments on "responsible" teenage lovers. "We just feel that marriage is not what legitimates sexual gratification," the Rev. John Carey, who chaired the drafting committee, observed.

Reluctant to lose members by taking unpopular stands, the church with this report heads straight on into the body oil business. If Christianity had pursued popularity at its inception, in an equally licentious era, Christians would have been handing out sheets at the orgies.

Then there's Dear Abby, she to whom more Americans look for personal advice than any other. In a recent column, Abby published a letter from a Virginia gynecologist lauding a state law under which minors are entitled to information about birth control, abortion, and sexually transmitted disease without parental consent or knowledge. In guiding teens past the perilous shoals of puberty, "value judgments must be put aside," the doc declared.

Abby thanked her correspondent for his "kind and reassuring words," then suggested that teens in need of sex advice should consult Planned Parenthood. A mother called me recently to complain of an AIDS education course at her local high school, taught by the condom-mongers, wherein her teen-age son was advised that patronizing prostitutes is a matter of *choice*.

Abby is the perfect cultural chameleon. During the Fifties, she was gung-ho virginity and parental discipline. Today, she's open, non-judgmental.

But strive as she does to be "now," even Abby is behind the times. Enter Pam Smart, Miss Value-Free of 1991. A public school teacher in Derry, New Hampshire, the twenty-three-year-old heavy-metal fan recruited her student lover and his two friends to kill her husband for his life insurance. Smart met the lads in a drug awareness course she taught, called "Project Self-Esteem," part of the value-neutral curricula infesting our public schools. Here students are instructed that the *decision-making-process* is far more important than the conclusion reached. We can only hope Greg Smart's killers felt good about themselves.

Which is not to say that adultery leads inexorably to family homicide. If it did, we'd be knee deep in blood. But there is a connection between sexual morality and virtue generally. It is no coincidence that the same Decalogue which demands fidelity also prohibits murder and theft.

The sexual revolution was intended as a minor adjustment. We wanted a society where we could dispense with puritanical codes (because, we were constantly told, humans have these needs which are impossible to deny) but keep the rest of traditional morality. While perambulating the primrose path, we would still be a nation of kind, caring, honest individuals.

It simply doesn't work that way. Is the person who cheats on a spouse more or less likely to lie, steal, and adopt a thoroughly cynical attitude toward existence? Will promiscuous teens be faithful in marriage, assuming they even get that far?

Sexual morality isn't only about what happens behind closed doors, between *consenting adults*. It's also about self-control, playing by the rules, treating others as ends not means.

"Value judgments must be put aside" isn't a formula for the salvation of a society, but a prescription for its extinction.

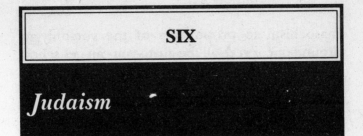

SIX

Judaism

Yom Kippur spirit vs. our culture
(19 September 1988)

To the haunting strains of the Kol Nidre,
Yom Kippur—the Day of Atonement—will begin
tomorrow at sunset.

For Jews, it is a day imbued with deep significance—a day of marathon synagogue services (of
prayers and hymns), a day of fasting and general
abstention from physical pleasure, a day for afflicting the spirit.

Each year it becomes increasingly apparent
to me that Yom Kippur provides a stark contrast
to this nation's dominant cultural ethos. The sym-
bolism of the high holy day runs completely contrary to the spirit of the times.

In America, not denial but self-indulgence is
the norm. "Bigger, better, more," Madison Avenue screams at us. "What! You're satisfied with
your four-year-old family car, when you could be
driving this sexy new, sports car, with ABS disc
brakes, independent suspension, six way seats, and
landau tops? You're not serious!"

The very notion of abstinence, of denying
appetites however briefly, must seem like insane

105

masochism to proponents of the you-only-go-around-once/grab-all-the-gusto-you-can-get school of life. Even more bizarre, from this perspective, is Yom Kippur's theme of sin and repentance. For modernists, this is truly an archaic notion, the disciples of Freud having long ago psychologized sin out of existence.

If no one is really responsible for their actions (a basic tenet of the creed), if conduct is molded by environment or heredity, how can we speak of right and wrong? There are merely random molecules, colliding mindlessly in space, producing desirable or less desirable effects.

As well as individual accountability, Yom Kippur speaks to collective responsibility. A central component of the synagogue services is the Al Het confessional prayer, in which members of the congregation declare in unison their guilt for a long list of offenses (greed, envy, lust, etc.), most of which the vast majority, in fact, did not commit.

Unlike radical individualism, Judaism recognizes the intimate connection between personal conduct and societal conventions. The individual is surely responsible for his actions; but so too, to a lesser extent, is the community.

In assessing our collective liability, we must ask if we, as a community, established appropriate standards. When we saw others going astray, did we try to dissuade them? Did we set a good example?

At the core of the Day of Atonement is the concept of God as the arbiter of human action: passing judgments, meting out punishments and rewards. On Rosh Hashanah, it is said, each person's fate is inscribed in the Book of Life, according to his merits. On Yom Kippur, the book is sealed. The period between the two holy days is a time of reflection and repentance, during which the ill decree may yet be reversed.

For the sophisticates who, if they still believe in a creator at all, perceive him as a remote, impersonal being, aloof from the affairs of man, such a doctrine is totally alien. How can man appeal to a detached deity? The Jewish concept of God involved in history, shaping our destiny, must be almost incomprehensible.

None of these concepts (sin, repentance, individual and collective responsibility, God as judge and redeemer) is unique to Judaism, although—as the first of the monotheistic faiths—it pioneered each of them. Indeed, these ideas permeate Judeo-Christian religion, giving rise to the moral genius of the West.

Our distance from them, as a nation and culture, is a catastrophe whose consequences are now only remotely discerned. The roots of our drug problem, teen alcoholism, the crisis of illegitimacy, of a million abortions annually, criminality in our inner cities, and family dissolution lie in our abandonment of the doctrines decreed at Sinai.

Our society can yet be saved, if we but have the wisdom and courage to accept these sacred truths. For instance, a return to a God-centered existence would do more to combat the scourge of drug abuse than all of the advertising, celebrity appeals, and government expenditures combined.

On this Yom Kippur, our culture should stand as the chief penitent, promising reformed behavior, beseeching forgiveness—despite its complete unworthiness to do so.

Assimilated Jews, liberal politics:
They never learn
(7 September 1992)

Those who are waiting for the Jewish electorate to come to its senses and abandon the reflex
liberalism so inimical to its interests will wait in
vain. Shrimp will learn to whistle "Hava Nagilah"
before American Jews escape the liberal ghetto.

A friend who's active in Jewish-Republican
politics is thoroughly frustrated by what he's hearing from the community in the wake of the GOP
convention. "When those Republicans in Hous-
ton started talking about God, it gave me the
willies," a prominent Jewish leader told him.

It takes an understanding of authentic Judaism to appreciate the irony of this remark. The
Jewish mission is precisely to talk about God, to
make humanity aware of His dominion, to remind
us of the necessity of God-based ethics. Absent
that, there is no logical reason for the continued
existence of the Jewish people.

Largely ignorant of the teachings of their faith,
the political imperative of Jewish voters apparently is to promote every ism—feminism, environmentalism, welfarism—save Judaism.

Excepting blacks, Jews are the most liberal
voting bloc. In 1988, 70 percent of Jews cast their
ballots for Michael Dukakis. Jewish support for
the Democratic nominee exceeded his vote among
the unemployed (65 percent), union households
(64 percent), Hispanics (66 percent), and even his
fellow Greeks (55 percent).

The only bright spot in this otherwise dreary
picture is Orthodox Jewry. The president carried

Orthodox neighborhoods in New York by anywhere from 72 percent to 86 percent of the vote.
In an article in *Moment Magazine*, Alan M. Fisher
advises Republicans to pray for the success of the
ba'al teshuva movement, the phenomenon of
young Jews from assimilated backgrounds choosing to become Orthodox.

The schizophrenia of Jewish politics was su-
perbly illustrated during the Gulf War. Abandon-
ing their historic pacifism, Jewish organizations
were eager to see the administration counter the
greatest threat to Israeli security in a generation—
the megalomaniacal ambitions of a man who threatened to unleash a second holocaust.

Yet the very same organizations for years had
urged defense cuts which, had they been enacted,
would have made Desert Storm impossible. This
year, the party whose congressional delegation
overwhelmingly opposed the war to stop Saddam
will once again be the overwhelming beneficiary
of Jewish votes, as will Bill Clinton, whose wife—as
head of the New World Foundation—gave money
to an organization that supports PLO front groups.

Liberals like Leonard Fein, founder of Moment, take pride in the paradox. Jewish voting
patterns are at variance with the rest of the white
electorate, because Jews put their values before
self-interest, they assert.

But there's nothing even remotely Jewish,
in a theological sense, about those values. Support
for abortion on demand, legitimizing homosexuality, and banishing religion from the public sphere
are the very antithesis of normative Judaism, as
can be seen in the pronouncements of groups like
the Orthodox Union, the Rabbinical Council of

America, and Agudath Israel, whose policies reflect the Torah ethos.

Jewish liberalism can only be explained as a matter of blind faith. Liberalism is the secular creed of the non-religious. Jews are perhaps the most secularized community in the nation. Only 11 percent of American Jews go to synagogue once a week, compared to the 42 percent of the general population that attends religious services on a weekly basis. The vast majority of American Jews are Jewishly illiterate, not knowing *halacha* (Jewish law) from *hummus* (a popular Israeli dish).

For those who've abandoned or—more precisely—never known traditional religion, liberalism frequently fills a void. It is the ersatz faith of 20th-century America, providing its followers with a world view, an explanation for the existence of evil (unbridled capitalism, militarism, sexism, religious fundamentalism), and a vision of salvation (the welfare state).

It gives its adherents a set of guiding principles—in the words of pop psychology, allowing them to feel good about themselves. Its dogma is comprehensive: Thou shalt raise taxes, spend more on the poor, enlarge the public sector, institute quotas for disadvantaged minorities, combat intolerance (religious values), cut defense spending, and bow down to the rain forest.

That Jewish voters cling tenaciously to this dogma in the face of massive evidence of its failure—a multigenerational welfare class, declining productivity, staggering deficit, and stifling bureaucracy—proves the commitment is based on faith, not reason. Believers to the end, American Jews may be the last acolytes to tend to the sacred flame of liberalism.

Kushner's God is yawn-inspiring
(November 1989)

Note to authors: Choosing a question for the title of your book entails certain risks. It may tempt a response that underscores the work's central irrelevance. Thus, one is inclined to respond to the title of Harold Kushner's latest book (*Who Needs God?*): Under your definition of the Deity, rabbi, absolutely no one.

Kushner, the spiritual leader of a suburban Boston temple, is becoming the Norman Vincent Peale of the Eighties. His first book, *When Bad Things Happen To Good People,* sold over two million copies.

Typical of liberal theologians, the rabbi has endeavored to squeeze all of the substance out of his faith. His is the god of the deists, a not-so-supreme being who created the universe, then let it go its merry way. This god can inspire, but (much like the head of state in a constitutional monarchy) cannot or will not intervene in our affairs.

Kushner sees Scriptures the way the Supreme Court views the Constitution: subject to highly imaginative interpretation. At one point the rabbi speculates: "Moses may have gotten his ideas about morality from the same place that Shakespeare got his poetry and Mozart his music, but the process surpasses my understanding." A frank admission, this.

He implies the concepts of heaven and hell are not to be taken literally. The former means our good deeds live after us, the latter, the opposite (cold comfort for the soul which hungers for survival beyond the shroud). These modernist musings bear about as much resemblance to normative Judaism as the sex novels of Father Andrew Greeley do to Catholic doctrine.

According to Kushner, the business of religion isn't about salvation or truth or God's will, but helping us to cope. "The purpose of religion is not to explain God or to please God, but to help us meet some of our most basic human needs." Again, "religious ritual and religious belief on which it is based cannot avert danger, but it can help us to face it bravely . . ."

In other words, trying to comprehend God and do His will are irrelevant. For Kushner, religion serves the same function as psychoanalysis— allowing people to sort out their emotions, overcome fears, and face painful situations.

If the rabbi has very little to say about God, it's because the Master of the Universe assumes a relatively insignificant role in his theology (that of a well-wishing, but detached, observer). Nonetheless, one gets the impression that by "God" Kushner means our collective consciousness or some such sociological construct.

It's quite logical for liberal theology to arrive at this point. Since the origin of Scriptures is man's creative capacity, God is unknowable and there are no theological certainties—meeting our emotional needs is all that matters. One can imagine the modernists' God inquiring of the children of Israel, assembled at the foot of Mount Sinai: "Are you comfortable with not stealing?"

The problem with this functional theology is that it leads to a religion of convenience. Thus liberal divines in the National Council of Churches and the mainline denominations can condone abortion, premarital sex, and homosexuality on utilitarian grounds: Since people are going to do it anyway, why make them feel guilty about it? Love and freedom become the highest values, discipline and sacrifice the enemy.

Not surprisingly, Kushner is concerned about the revival of traditional religion which, he believes, is based on "a fear of freedom, a fear of making choices." "In its more benign form, it gives us people who are shaped by their religious commitment into rigid, judgmental, humorless souls."

"Rigidity" means a belief in absolutes. Being "judgmental" is the awful act of informing sinners that they are sinful. These are the ultimate evils for a modernist theologian. Having no absolutes themselves, they have a pathological fear of certainty. Rendering judgements is the very opposite of being supportive, which tops their agenda.

In the final analysis, utilitarian theology fails the test of usefulness. People do need God—a god who cares, a god who saves, a god who is intimately involved with his creation, not the pallid creature who inhabits Harold Kushner's books. Kushner's conception of God evokes not awe but ennui.

Does Judaism Have a Mission to Humanity?

(Speech to 13th anniversary dinner of Yeshiva Migdal Torah, Chicago, May 21, 1992.)

Let us admit it at the outset: American Jews are a parochial community. When we speak of "Jewish issues," we mean Israel, anti-Semitism, intermarriage, and assimilation. This perspective is perhaps quite natural, given our minority status and unhappy history. To rephrase Rabbi Hillel's famous dictum: If we are not for ourselves, who will be? But we neglect at our peril the second half of the sage's equation: If we are only for ourselves, what are we?

We live in a country where Jews comprise less than 3 percent of the population, a figure which sadly is declining. We inhabit a planet where Jews barely register on demographic scales, nearly lost among 4 billion people. As the tragic events which unfolded in Crown Heights last September demonstrate all too clearly, everything that happens among the non-Jewish inhabitants of America, and the world, has a profound impact on Jews.

I would like to take a few minutes to explore a theme that has always intrigued me, one which I believe has a direct bearing on the future of our community: Does Judaism have anything at all to say to gentiles? In other words, to put it somewhat dramatically: Does Judaism have a mission to humanity?

That Judaism is unique among the world's major religions in not seeking converts often leads to the misconception that ours is a parochial faith, concerned with the spiritual welfare of its own, and no one else.

History amply refutes this charge. During the biblical period, Jews had a keen sense of their destiny. Judaism came into existence to challenge all of the cherished assumptions of the pagan world: polytheism, unrestrained sensuality, rule of the strong, and exploitation of the weak.

There is but one God, Jews proclaimed. He is indivisible, incorporeal, and all-powerful, the universal deity, creator and master of the universe, whose principal demands are justice and holiness.

The Torah discloses that Israel's deliverance from Egypt was meant to demonstrate His omnipotence and compassion to all of humanity. In his commentary on Torah, the great nineteenth century leader of German Jewry, Rabbi Sampson Raphael Hirsch, explained: "It was not only to educate this people to be Thy people; the enlightenment and instruction of the other nations was also an essential objective of this whole miraculous redemption."

Mosaic law was intended for the Jewish people but with profound implications for the rest of humanity. Indeed, our tradition tells us that the first ten *mitzvot* (commandments) were given in seventy languages, so that all the nations of the earth could understand them.

The message of the prophets, including Jonah's admonition to Nineveh, was often directed at the gentile nations.

Historians inform us that, due to the popularity of Judaism in the ancient world, one out of every ten citizens of the Roman Empire was a Jew. Others, while never formally converting, studied

the wisdom of Torah and practiced the humane
precepts of Jewish law. The Holy Temple in Jerusalem had a special courtyard where non-Jews
brought sacrifices.

As it was in the beginning, so will it be in the
end. The Torah promises that in the days of
Moshiach (the Messiah) the law will go forth from
Jerusalem to encompass the earth. During most of
the Diaspora, while Jews often had a substantial
impact on the cultures in which they lived, persecution and the constant struggle for survival caused
them to look inward.

In modern times, the pendulum began to
swing back. Colonial America was heavily influenced by Jewish concepts: the dignity of the individual, equality before the law, a written legal code,
a nation without a monarch governed by the will
of Providence. The founding fathers identified
closely with the children of Israel, believing they
too had come into the wilderness to escape oppression, eventually establishing a new nation dedicated to freedom and justice.

So strong was this attachment that Cotton
Mather, the noted Puritan theologian, wanted to
make Hebrew the official language of the Massachusetts Bay Colony. In the colonial era, children
often were given names from the Jewish Bible:
Moses, Levi, Jeremiah, etc. A verse from our Bible,
from *Va-Yikra* (Leviticus), was chosen for the inscription on Philadelphia's Liberty Bell (which
tolled to announce the adoption of the Declaration of Independence): "Proclaim Liberty Throughout the Land, Unto All the Inhabitants Thereof."

The U.S. Constitution is the last link in a
chain stretching back to Sinai. Thus it is no exag-

geration to say that without ancient Israel, there would have been no United States of America.

But this is far from Judaism's only contribution to the modern world. Today, most of mankind follows the teachings of Judaism or of individual Jews, however imperfectly comprehended or even distorted these may be. Of course there's Judaism and its offshoots: Christianity and Islam.

But all of the principal political/cultural creeds which have impacted on the twentieth century—democracy, humanism, psychoanalysis, capitalism, and socialism—were shaped by the Jewish world view.

Regrettably, in the modern age the message which Jews have brought to humanity too often has been secular in nature (advocacy for utopianism, feminism, sexual liberation, and internationalism) instead of an authentically Jewish message, to the great detriment of Jews and non-Jews alike. As has been noted, not without a sense of irony, those Jews that the world should hear from most, it actually hears from least, and those it should hear from least it hears from far too often.

Today religious Jews confront a world in the process of moral disintegration, a world not so very different from the one which Judaism encountered at its inception. In the modern industrialized nations, gross immorality seems to be the order of the day. Promiscuity, perversion, pornography, violence, and drug abuse all are rampant—Sodom and Gomorah with cable television and alternative lifestyles.

In America, various studies disclose that the average girl loses her virginity at age sixteen. Three thousand adolescents become pregnant each day; 80 percent are unmarried. More than two million teen-agers have some form of venereal disease. One and one-half million abortions are performed in this country each year.

In 1991, there were more than twenty-five thousand murders in America—an all time high. President Bush put it in rather stark terms when he said: "During the first few days of the ground offensive (in the Persian Gulf), more Americans were killed in some American cities than at the entire Kuwaiti front." Between 1984 and 1988, the rate of teen-agers arrested for murder doubled.

Drug use is epidemic. One in ten Americans use an illicit drug regularly. There are six million cocaine addicts in this nation. Among the young, the problem is entrenched. Of those eighteen to twenty-five years of age, 22 percent smoke marijuana. A quarter of all high-school students use a narcotic substance at least once a month.

A few years ago, a UCLA psychologist interviewed 288 freshman, asking each if he would commit rape if he knew he could get away with it. One out of four said they would. (On the bright side, after graduation most will probably rape the stock market, the Treasury, or the depositors of a savings and loan institution instead of committing a more personal act of violence.)

Please understand these aren't young men from deprived backgrounds, scions of crime-breeding slums, but the children of affluence who, in most cases, are of above average intelligence, well-educated by contemporary standards and have never wanted for any material comfort.

Unfortunately—for both themselves and the society on which they soon will be inflicted—no one ever bothered to tell them not to trust their instincts; that right and wrong are universal and objective (and not subject to their whims); that human nature is weak—as the Talmud says: From birth a man's heart is inclined to evil; that it's usually easier to do the wrong thing (which gratifies both our senses and our egos) than the right thing; that decency requires a great deal of self-discipline; that virtue must be carefully, painstakingly inculcated—as a friend of mine is fond of saying: it's easier to make a good neurosurgeon than a good person; that it's wrong to hurt people, even if you're not caught; that in harming others we diminish ourselves; that ultimately we are accountable for our actions.

Clearly, mankind needs this Jewish message as it has never needed it before.

What then is our mission? To lead uniquely Jewish lives, lives dedicated to charity (*tsadaka*), piety, and virtue, to living the tenets of Jewish law (*halachah*).

To teach by our example. Words are increasingly cheap (witness a Jimmy Swaggart, a Jim Baker, or a Bill Clinton); it's actions that make the strongest impression. Like a pebble thrown into the middle of a lake, Torah Jews can have a ripple effect on those around them, just by acting the way people should, but rarely do behave.

To testify to God's presence in the world. According to the Ibn Ezra, the Sa'adiah Gaon observed that the Jew will be known by how well he keeps the *Shabbat*. One of the Torah verses concerning Sabbath observance says: "So that you shall know that I am the Lord your God." Asked the Sa'adiah Gaon, "Who has to know this?" And he answered: the non-Jew.

In other words, every time a Jew keeps the *Shabbat* (every time he refrains from creative work on that day) it reminds non-Jews of His sovereignty, that there is a God who created the world and that he has certain requirements of us.

The same could be said of many of the *mitzvot* (commandments). When I started keeping kosher, I stopped eating the food in our company cafeteria and brought my lunch instead. I refrained from dining out with colleagues, unless it was at a kosher restaurant. Quite naturally, my friends and co-workers were curious.

When they discovered my motivation, they were impressed by the fact that here was a person who was willing to do something—even at the cost of inconvenience and modest sacrifice—because he believed it was God's will. A number began wondering if perhaps there wasn't something God wanted them to do. It might not be keeping kosher, but there must be something they could do to show their gratitude for His blessings, to connect more closely to the source of their lives. In a nation where the average individual thinks about God twice a year—if that, for many twice in a lifetime (when a loved one is sick or in danger)—may I suggest that this is not a bad thing.

Our mission includes reaching out to assimilated, alienated Jews. Obviously, there can be no message without messengers. Judaism understands something that revolutionary movements throughout history have never grasped: If you want to change the world, you must begin by changing yourself.

Mitzvot like *kashrut* and *Shabbat* observance aren't just rituals but methods of instructing ourselves and those around us in the ways of righteousness.

Most specifically, to stand up for morality, to point out the social consequences (the suffering, both physical and psychological) of the decline of traditional values; to work to strengthen the family—the indispensable building block of society.

The fact that we're not a proselytizing faith, that unlike other religions we do not seek converts, makes our message all the more credible. We're not saying to the rest of humanity: You have to become a Jew to have a share of *olam haba*, of the world to come, rather you have to be good. We're not telling the gentiles "be a Jew," but "be a mensche!"

In recent years, a number of Torah sages have declared that it is a *mitzvah* (commandment) for Jews to teach non-Jews the Noahide laws. This is the legal code presented to the sons of Noah after the flood (which includes prohibitions against murder, theft, sexual immorality, and the mandate to establish courts of law to dispense justice) and, unlike the Torah, is incumbent on all of humanity. By the way, if you think gentiles already have this because it's part of their Bible too, you haven't been reading the newspaper lately.

A Jewish leader who is acutely cognizant of Judaism's universal mission is Lord Immanuel Jakobovits, former chief rabbi of the United Kingdom. The first rabbi to be elevated to the House of Lords, Rabbi Jakobovits became a moral leader of Britain, the nation's foremost clerical champion of normative values. When the Church of England issued a paper condemning Thatcher's free market policies as harmful to the poor, the rabbi countered with his own statement stressing the ennobling quality of work. When the church debated changing its position on homosexuality, Rabbi Jakobovits warned of the dangers of condoning immorality in the name of compassion, in his monograph on AIDS.

In his 1966 book, *Journal of a Rabbi*, Lord Jakobovits set forth the case for Jewish moral engagement in ringing tones: "In the gigantic struggle, which will determine human as well as Jewish survival, between the forces of morality founded on religion and of crass materialism fed by godlessness, there can be but one legitimate choice for Jews if they are not to renounce their prophetic heritage as the people who were told: 'Ye are My witnesses.'"

Even if we didn't have this divine mandate, self-interest alone should impel us accept the assignment. If the twentieth century (the century of secret police, Auschwitz, and gulags) has taught us anything, it is the grave danger to Jews when a significant segment of humanity casts off moral constraints in favor of utilitarian values.

One of my favorite Jewish stories is set in Europe a century ago and concerns the rabbi who was travelling by coach from one town to another. At one point the rabbi's driver discovered he had forgotten to bring along feed for the horses.

"I'll just stop along the road and take some grain from a farmer's field," the driver said, asking the rabbi to keep watch and let him know if anyone saw him, so that he could make a fast getaway.

While the driver was thus occupied, the rabbi ran up behind him shouting "One sees!" The driver hurriedly got back into the coach and drove away with the rabbi.

A few miles down the road, he looked back and saw that no one was following them. Angry, for he thought the rabbi was trying to make a fool of him, he berated his passenger. "Rabbi," the coachman hotly protested, "you said someone saw me, but there's no one around. Are you playing tricks on me?" In answer, the rabbi pointed toward Heaven and repeated his admonition: "One sees!" The driver was filled with shame.

This, ladies and gentlemen, is the essence of the Jewish mission: to persuade humanity that someone indeed is watching us, one to whom we all are ultimately accountable. On the success or failure of this mission the fate of the world hinges.

SEVEN

AIDS/Sex Education

Legion of latex recruits in school
(5 December 1991)

Condom distribution in public schools has nothing to do with disease control and everything to do with normalizing a sexual ethic. That simple fact is all you need to know about the prophylactic assault on America's school children.

An AP wirephoto caught my eye. It showed two children, Joe Temperino and his girlfriend, Helene Patterson, posed before the gates of Brooklyn's John Dewey High School. The teens held aloft their school supplies—a packet of Trojan-Enz.

Last week, New York launched its condom campaign in the public schools. In one of life's tantalizing little ironies, the drive kicked off at John Dewey High, named for the pragmatist philosopher who rejected eternal values in favor of secular salvation, to be achieved by educational indoctrination. Somewhere in humanist heaven, Dewey is doing handstands.

Closer to home, Cambridge and Falmouth, Mass., both have condomized their schools. In Boston, a junior high student stated that Mayor Ray

125

Flynn—father of six—was naive in suggesting that condoms promote sexual experimentation.

New York Chancellor of Schools Joseph Fernandez, who opposed any form of parental consent, allowed that while the public may argue about "philosophical niceties," "at the bottom of the debate is whether kids are going to live or kids are going to die." In other words, the decision to introduce fifteen-year-old girls to the physical and psychological perils of premarital sex is a "philosophical nicety" which parents will be permitted to discuss but not influence.

The latest contraceptive crusade is based on the following dubious assumptions:

1) That New York City high-school students have no idea of where to obtain condoms; 2) that teens with their $150 hightops can't afford condoms; 3) that children whose vocabulary would make Andrew Dice Clay blush are too shy to purchase them in drugstores. If you believe any of the foregoing, your reality quotient is such that you immediately qualify for an administrative position in the New York public school system.

If our concern is AIDS, Joey and Helene don't need the latex devices. Assuming neither is an intravenous drug user nor the sex partner of a homosexual, their risk of contracting the contagion approaches zero.

In the current issue of *Commentary* magazine, Michael Fumento informs us that out of 188,348 diagnosed cases of AIDS in this country, whites who say they acquired the disease through heterosexual contact account for exactly 727—less than one-half of 1 percent. In 1988, the AMA estimated one's chances of getting AIDS from a single encounter with someone not in a high risk category as one in five million. As an AIDS preventive, Joey and Helene need condoms about as much as they need to be immunized against the bite of the African tsetse fly.

Which is just as well. Were they at risk, condoms wouldn't help them much. Read the disclaimer on a package of Trojan's finest *"may help reduce* the risk of catching or spreading *many* sexually transmitted diseases."

Condoms leak; condoms slip; condoms break. As a birth control device, they fail anywhere from 15 to 30 percent of the time. For AIDS prevention, they're even less reliable.

While AIDS may not be a problem for them, there are a lot of other nasty infections Joe and Helene can pick up from the biological experiment being urged upon them. Since 1983, the rate of syphilis in their age group has increased fifteen times. In a viral sea, condoms are a deflated life jacket.

Dr. Theresa Crenshaw of the Presidential AIDS Commission did a straw poll at a conference of over eight hundred sexologists. How many recommend condoms for their clients, she inquired? Most hands went up. "I (then) asked them if they had available the partner of their dreams, and knew that person carried a (venereal) virus, would they have sex, depending on a condom for protection? No one raised their hand."

Now the legion of latex is neither ignorant nor stupid. It knows how the disease is spread and the degrees of risk for various groups. It has read the studies on condom failure rates. In short, its advocacy is philosophical, not medicinal.

And yet, for public consumption, the same people who will strenuously maintain that ciga-

rette advertising sends a powerful message of societal approval to adolescents will declare with a
perfectly straight face that there is no moral content to condom distribution in the public schools.

When a school nurse or health teacher be-
stows a prophylactic on a juvenile, there is an
implicit message attached to the act: That we adults
know you kids can't control yourselves, so please
be careful. That what's really important here (other
than philosophical niceties) isn't ethics, but taking
the proper precautions.

School days, school days, good old lubricated
latex days. By sacrificing morality for safety, we
shall have neither.

AIDS educator raises parents' hackles
(21 May 1992)

A self-styled "hot and sexy" AIDS educator
may be the best thing to happen to private education since Wisconsin State Rep. Polly Williams
(she of tuition vouchers for inner-city students).
By turning our schools into slime pits, AIDS education and condom distribution will prove an in-
calculable boon to the voucher movement.

Suzi Landolphi raised parental hackles when
her ninety-minute AIDS sideshow hit the
Chelmsford, Mass., High School. Landolphi's bur-
lesque, presented at a mandatory assembly, included raunchy language, stretching a condom
above the head of a male student (presumably to
prove that one size fits all) and imparting such
vital information as the observation that orgasm
relieves tension and is "ten times stronger than valium."

During a New Hampshire engagement, the
creative communicator danced in the aisle with a

male student and told the guys: "You have hundreds of words for your private parts. I think it's because you're always talking to it."

Landolphi's routine is only one of the innovative approaches public schools are using to spread the gospel of safe sex.

In Swampscott, Mass., students as young as eleven brought home a dandy little book called *Risky Times*, which explains, in graphic detail, how to have anal and oral sex. (Something every eleven-year-old wants to know.) The work of a local pornographer? In a manner of speaking. The book was presented to grades six through twelve by the town's school system.

In New York City, the board of health distributes a pamphlet apprising students of their "right (constitutional? God-given?) to decide to have sex and who to have it with," while volunteers from the Gay Men's Health Crisis hand out condoms in the classrooms.

Washington, DC, Mayor Sharon Pratt Kelly just announced plans to condomize that city's schools. We know parents will have coronary seizures over this, admits school superintendent Franklin Smith, "but we have to convince them that this is an investment in their future"—much like the purchase of a coffin, no doubt?

For the public education establishment, "convincing" consists of keeping parents in the dark (but most of all we gotta hide it from the folks) or treating them like freaks when they object to this moral anarchy in the name of disease prevention.

Chelmsford parents were never notified of Landolphi's peep show. When she performed in New Hampshire, parents were barred from the auditorium by a principal who said he "didn't want any scenes." Although New York State allows parents to withdraw their children from AIDS programs, educators interpret the option as narrowly as possible, holding: "The school is not under an affirmative obligation to inform parents of their rights. . . ."

When the L.A. Unified School District decided to conduct a series of public forums on its proposed condom crusade, officials were amazed by the vehemence of the response. Taken aback, they simply dismissed the protestors as right-wing kooks and religious fanatics and proceeded with the program. Parents in the town of Falmouth, Mass., collected three thousand signatures against condom dispensing machines in the high-school boys room. The school committee responded by voting to extend the program to the junior high level.

Fostered by hysteria, AIDS education proceeds from fallacious assumptions: "Kids will do it anyway. Safety first."

But the average teen is far less erogenously involved than they would have us believe. In a 1986 Harris Poll, 72 percent of girls aged twelve to eighteen had not engaged in intercourse. The term "sexually experienced" is misleading; 20 percent of teens fifteen to seventeen so classified have had intercourse only once.

Cheer up, Planned Parenthood. AIDS education and condom distribution will boost these statistics. A 1986 study by the Alan Guttmacher Institute found that fourteen-year-old girls who have had comprehensive sex education are 40 percent more likely to have sex than those who were deprived of such erotic instruction. Another study disclosed that plying kids with contraceptives increases sexual activity by 50 percent.

Condoms, the prophylactic paladins of AIDS mythology, have a 15 percent failure rate for contraception. For AIDS prevention, they are practically useless. The virus is 450 times smaller than a sperm, hence better able to permeate the rubber barrier. Latex gloves three times as thick as condoms have leaked blood.

When educators get away with one outrage, they up the ante. First sex education, then AIDS education, then condom distribution. What next, combination classroom-motel rooms, so safe sex can be properly monitored by concerned educators?

In the midst of this pedagogic psychosis, California prepares to vote on vouchers for private education, proponents having collected nearly one million signatures to put the measure on the ballot. While the education lobby raves that this will destroy public schools, they are working overtime, albeit unwittingly, to convince the average parent that sending their children to a public school is comparable to consigning them to a brothel. Suzi Landolphi, take a bow.

EIGHT

Media

Where's media's spirit, soul?
(25 December 1989)

In disparaging religion, Hollywood believes it is helping to free humanity from emotional repression and intolerance. In reality, it is liberating our less elevated instincts.

In the January issue of its newsletter, the American Family Association published an inventory of prime time smears of Christianity over the past year. In almost every program in which they appeared, clergy and laity were depicted as sinister hypocrites, bigots, or boobs.

Here's a brief sampling of TV's gentle treatment of the followers of Jesus, as described in the AFA's *Journal*: "Jan. 31: NBC's 'In The Heat of The Night' revolved around an adulterous preacher in fictional Sparta, Mississippi . . . Feb. 17: ABC's 'Just The Ten of Us' continued its negative portrayal of the show's Catholic priest, presenting him as a buffoon . . . March 19-20: ABC's 'The Women of Brewster Place' contained the stereotypical Christian hypocrites including an adulterous preacher and a Christian woman who is mean and harsh. Sept. 15: CBS's 'Unholy Matrimony . . . In the movie, the Rev. Samuel Cory ran a chain of bordellos, and also helped his bigamist friend murder his wives . . . Oct. 9: NBC's 'Dream Date' had a Christian woman who watches a healing evangelist on TV and is depicted as a demented nymphomaniac."

No other group is so consistently maligned on prime time television. These defamatory portrayals betray a deep-seated hostility. Perhaps TBS mogul Ted Turner articulated the unspoken values of his fellow network executives when he confided to the TV critic of the *Dallas Morning News*: "Christianity is a religion for losers."

"I've had a few drinks and a few girlfriends and if that's going to put me in hell, then so be it," says Turner. This is typical of the media mindset, which views the Judeo-Christian ethic as a code for killjoys. It's time to assign the anachronistic creed to the dustbin of history and proceed with our happiness agenda, the entertainment industry seems to be saying.

One who certainly endorsed these sentiments was the late H.L. Mencken. No other writer did more to shape media iconoclasm than the Sage of Baltimore, who taught the lumpen intelligentsia to snicker at religion.

In Sunday school he learned that ". . . the Christian faith was full of palpable absurdities, and the Christian God preposterous," Mencken wrote. How the foe of Babbitry loved to lampoon fundamentalists. "They swarm in the towns, inflamed by their pastors. . . . They are thick in the mean streets behind the gas works. They are everywhere that learning is too heavy a burden for mortal minds. . . . ," the Norman Lear precursor proclaimed.

Mencken's deities were Darwin, Huxley, and Nietzche—which is to say: evolution and the cult of the dionysian individualist. Like Turner and his ilk, he viewed religion as a dark superstition, the enemy of reason and progress, the creed of puritans tormented by the thought that "someone, somewhere is happy."

As the world learned with the recent release of his diaries, Christians weren't the only victims of Mencken's rancor. The prototypical media debunker was an antediluvian racist and a vicious anti-Semite. Blacks had the mentality of children, while Jews were crude, unethical moneygrubbers, Mencken confided to his diary.

He was gleeful when the only Jew in his country club died and the membership determined not to admit another. Even after the war, when the horrors of the Holocaust were documented beyond denial, Mencken still railed against American intervention. Perhaps he reasoned that at least Hitler's six million victims would not be joining his country club.

Mencken was the quintessential modernist—the supreme egotist, who lived by his own lights. Without a belief in man's supernatural origins, it's easy to fall into the fallacy of racial superiority.

Despite his wit and erudition, Mencken ended his days a bitter man, as contemptible a bigot as any of the "booboisie" he satirized.

A cautionary note to my media colleagues: Ridiculing religion may be great fun, but it does not a better society make. The individual released from the very necessary constraints of ethical monotheism doesn't become noble in his savagery, merely savage.

Beauty and the Beverly Hills beasts
(5 March 1992)

The public is starved for values in the entertainment media. Witness two phenomena: a song
from the Fifties and an animated feature show-
ered with well-deserved honors.

Disney's *Beauty and the Beast* is the first animated film to be nominated for an Academy Award
for Best Picture, a testament to its popularity if
not a change of heart in Hollywood.

Within a week of that nomination, Natalie
Cole and "Unforgettable" dominated the Grammy
Awards, winning in the top three categories. With
all of the consciousness-annihilating, screeching
garbage that fills the airwaves—Madonna fondling
herself, rap odes to date rape, primal scream
melodies—what cops the music industry's most
prestigious prize but a sweet, sentimental love
ballad, straight out of the era of ponytails and
penny-loafers.

Beauty and the Beast has everything Hollywood
ordinarily doesn't have the guts, brains, or heart
to put into a contemporary film. Besides that very
special Disney magic—marvelous animation, music to sweep you away—this fairy tale set to song
has all of the right values: courage, compassion,
self-sacrifice.

Maybe I'm reading too much into a cartoon,
but I detect an interesting metaphor here, one
which would warm the hearts of conservative social critics like George Gilder.

In the story, woman's love tames the beast in
man. The selfish prince is given a physical form to
match his inner ugliness. The well-named Belle,
whose external beauty reflects narmony within, in

teaching him to care for more than himself, transforms the monster into real royalty.

Would that the beasts of Beverly Hills were as easily altered. The motion picture industry is committing slow suicide. In 1991, the number of movie tickets sold hit a fifteen-year low. An article in *Variety* reports the summer box office off 25 percent, video sales down 6 percent.

Increasingly movie audiences are homogeneous, composed almost exclusively of kids who have nothing better to do on a Saturday night and few critical faculties.

Consider the other "Best Picture" nominees: *Bugsy, JFK, Prince of Tides, Silence of the Lambs*. Is this the best Hollywood has to offer?

Last year's releases were typical of the cinematic sludge that sullies the screen: a suave cannibal (the Jeffrey Dahmer chic), homicidal housefraus off on crime spree. Oliver Stone's latest paranoid delusion (the Kennedy assassination according to William Kunstler), megagore from muscleman Ah-nod, Robin Williams getting funky with the homeless, a trio of big budget gangster movies (*Mobsters, Billy Bathgate, Bugsy*)—celebrations of social pathology all.

Look at the faces of people exiting the average showing. Are they smiling?

Joe Farah, editor of the media watch newsletter "Between the Lines," is blunt: "These movies aren't intended for enjoyment or inspiration. They're meant to provoke emotions, and very seldom is the intended reaction joy or hope, as was true of movies of the '40s and '50s."

I put the question to Charlton Heston, whom I had the pleasure of meeting recently: Why doesn't Hollywood make inspirational movies anymore?

Films like *Chariots of Fire* come along once in a
decade.

"In this town," says Heston, "Nobody wants
to take risks. People are afraid of their reputa-
tions. They're afraid that if they make a movie
with old-fashioned values, people will laugh at
them."

While this may be true in some cases, there is
more involved. What you see on the big screen,
and to a lesser extent on the small screen, reflects
the mind-set of the pseudo-intellectuals who make
the movies: pessimism, nihilism, cynicism, despair—
the view from the gutter.

Because they have nothing to say that the
average American wants to hear, they concentrate
on spectacle: special effects, nudity, simulated sex
(Here is an industry that assumes its customers
have the predilections of dirty old men in trench
coats.), buckets of blood, and unadulterated sadism.

Robert De Niro rendered a bravura performance in *Cape Fear*, but so what? Did we really
need one of the most graphic rape scenes in cinematic history, where the rapist bites off part of
his victim's face?

And they wonder why people above the IQ
of junior-high skaters don't go to movies. Can't
they understand that Christians don't enjoy seeing their religion reviled; parents don't thrill to
images of children being molested; veterans aren't
delighted to see their country constantly represented as a force for evil in the world?

Much as I enjoyed *Beauty and the Beast*, it was,
after all, just a cartoon, an animated rose bloom-
ing on a dung heap. Its Oscar nomination is win-
dow dressing—a way of saying: "See, we're really

not wallowing in the pathological; we've even given a nod of the head to this delightful film." That's exactly what it is: tokenism for traditional values.

Timely message in old-time movie
(3 December 1989)

It's a Wonderful Life is indisputably the most popular Christmas movie on television, surpassing such perennial favorites as *Miracle on 34th Street*, *White Christmas*, and the various versions of Dickens' *A Christmas Carol*.

In the Boston area, I once counted twenty-seven showings of the Frank Capra classic, almost one a day, between Thanksgiving and Christmas.

This is no mean feat for a low-budget film that lost money during its original release in 1946. In a 1982 *Chicago Tribune* poll, readers rated it one of the most popular movies of all times, surpassing such blockbusters as *Star Wars* and *The Wizard of Oz*.

As a tribute to its success, it was remade as a TV movie in 1977. *It's a Wonderful Life* is available on videocassette for under $10, a sure sign of a movie's popularity, price being a factor of production. Ted Turner produced a colorized version, and the entire script is available in an oversized paperback.

The film's seasonal prominence is paradoxical. *It's a Wonderful Life* really has nothing to do with the Yuletide, though the climax is on Christmas Eve. It's not about religion, notwithstanding that an angel supplies the dramatic device by which the conflict is resolved.

The story line is not the stuff of high drama: a slight amount of romance, very little action. *It's a Wonderful Life* is the rather mundane tale of a smalltown guy (Jimmy Stewart) whose big dreams remain just that.

George Bailey's life is a series of reluctant sacrifices for his family, the depositors of the Bailey Building and Loan, and the citizens of Bedford Falls. He gives up college to send his brother to school, stays home to run the family business when the alternative is liquidation. He even forgoes his honeymoon to stop a bank run during the Depression.

His operation of the Building and Loan allows the citizens of Bedford Falls to realize their modest ambitions of home ownership and keeps Mr. Potter (the richest and—hiss, boo—meanest man in town) from getting a stranglehold on the community.

A crisis and impending disaster, brought on by misplaced funds, causes George to question the value of his life, even to contemplate suicide. Enter his guardian angel who validates his existence by showing him what life in Bedford Falls would be like if he'd never been born.

In this alternative universe, the world minus George Bailey, his wife is a timid old maid, his mother an embittered widow. His brother died in a sledding accident as a child. Because George wasn't there to pull him from the icy pond, his brother (as an adult) wasn't there to save the men on his aircraft carrier. With no one to oppose him, Mr. Potter turns Bedford Falls into Pottersville, a honky-tonk, Las Vegas hell.

As Clarence the Angel confides to a dazed George, after showing him this demonic vision: "Strange, isn't it? Each man's life touches so many other lives, and when he isn't around he leaves an awful hole, doesn't he?"

That's why we love this marvelous movie: It is a dramatic refutation of the notion that we are slaves of circumstance, cogs in the great machine of history, moving uncomprehendingly to a climax we can neither foresee nor avert.

In an increasingly impersonal, detached world—where people feel isolated, cut off even from their loved ones—this is an urgently-needed message: that we count. We may lead what appear to be ordinary, relatively insignificant lives, but in fact shape reality far more than we'll ever know.

Through our acts of kindness and devotion to duty, little by little we build a better world. By our contributions to social institutions (businesses, schools, churches, and charities), we help so many others, people we'll never know, generations yet unborn.

What a powerful statement for a generation hungry for affirmation. The film had little impact in the late Forties because people then didn't need its tidings. We had just confronted and overcome two crises, the Depression and World War II, and felt invulnerable.

Today its words of encouragement and good cheer are never more timely, which is why the film continues to win new audiences—to conquer hearts and hearten spirits—after nearly half a century.

Father really did know best
(25 June 1989)

I grew up with "Father Knows Best"—the wise, witty Fifties sitcom. When an institution I cherish is attacked, I must rise to its defense.

On Father's Day, the CBN Family Channel ran a "Father Knows Best" seven-hour marathon.

Episodes were interspersed with reminiscences of cast members. To mark the occasion, *TV Guide* carried a story in its June 17 edition ("After Father Knows Best, It Was Drugs, Jail, Depression").

After describing the apple-pie wholesomeness of the Anderson household (the show's fictional family), the author asks: "But was that really what we were like in pre-Vietnam, pre-Watergate, predrug America. . . ?" Far from it, the piece implies, by focusing on the scarred lives of the series' child stars.

All came from broken homes. Billy Gray (Bud) had a troubled adolescence and once spent forty-five days in jail on a marijuana charge. Lauren Chapin (Kathy) was an abused child who became addicted to heroin and speed after the show was canceled and did time for forging a check. Elinor Donahue (Betty) had a disastrous first marriage.

Here, the article seems to say, is the reality of Fifties America: ugliness, desperation, and social decay, lurking beneath the facade of happy family life. The article quotes a bitter Gray calling the show "a lie, a lie that was sold to the American people."

But wherein does the truth lie? The tragedy of three lives traumatized in adolescence is lamentable. Then again, Hollywood has never been a microcosm of middle-class normalcy. Al Jolson may have been the entertainment industry's last family man.

Show business tends to attract unstable individuals seeking escape from tormented lives in a world of make-believe. Children cast into this hazardous environment frequently develop emotional problems—witness the spate of recent tell-all autobiographies by former child stars.

The Bells of St. Mary's was a beautiful, inspirational movie. Yet in real life Bing Crosby (who played the kindly priest) was an alcoholic; Ingrid Bergman (the dedicated nun) was an adulteress. Does this in any way detract from a charming story with an uplifting message? Does it mean kindly priests and self-sacrificing nuns exist only in the imagination of scriptwriters?

Should art mirror existence or idealize it? Of course, "Father Knows Best" was fantasy. The average 1950s dad was no more Robert Young than the average World War II marine was John Wayne. But in the family portrait it painted of marital contentment, parental concern, and family cohesion, the series gave us something to aspire to.

Perhaps Young and Wyatt provided role models some youngsters couldn't find at home. Certainly they are better standards than the parade of geeks, neurotics, and narcissists Hollywood now bids youthful audiences to emulate.

Why the urge to debunk the 1950s? It is revisionism fueled by the need to persuade us that today's broken homes, drug abuse, high crime rates, and rampant alienation always existed ("You think it was better then? You're kidding yourself."), instead of the direct result of values our society has accepted in the past twenty-five years.

It is an obsession of people who bought the myths of the Sixties (including the delusion of limitless personal autonomy) and now are leading terribly unhappy lives. Thus they feel compelled to justify themselves by trying to convince us that what is now always was.

The Andersons of Maple Avenue, Springfield, U.S.A., may have been idealized, but they had their counterparts, in kind if not in degree, in

homes across the country when the series premiered. Much to our misfortune, their modern
mates often seem an endangered species.

When I mentioned "Father Knows Best" to a
friend of my fifteen-year-old daughter, a quiet child
whose parents divorced many years ago, she smiled
enthusiastically. She watched the series on reruns
and adored it. Perhaps, then, the Andersons'
Springfield is a landmark on the road back to the
real America.

New TV season makes a real killing
(24 August 1989)

Imagine a group of drug dealers making the
following appeal:

If you don't like narcotics—if you believe they
would have an adverse effect on the health/emo-
tional well-being of you and your family—then, by
all means, refrain from using them. But don't try
to circumvent the judgment of millions of adult
Americans. If enough people simply stop buying
addictive substances, drug trafficking will disap-
pear. Let the market decide.

Ridiculous, no? Yet this is precisely the theory
advanced by broadcast bigwigs against industrywide
standards to reduce the amount of sex and violence on television.

Earlier this month, the U.S. House of Repre-
sentatives passed a bill exempting the networks,
cable companies, and independent operators from
certain provisions of the Sherman Anti-Trust Act
to enable them to devise such a voluntary code.

Network executives—who have the motto
Mammon Uber Alles tattooed over their shriveled
hearts—reacted predictably. "The bottom line is

consumers vote on our programming several times every night when they hit their remote control button. If the public thinks there is too much sex on television or violence on television, the best way to get it off is not to watch it," says CBS Vice President Martin Franks. This from the very responsible folks who nightly dump metric tons of psychic waste in living rooms across the land. Between the ages of six and eighteen, the average American youth will spend sixteen thousand hours in front of a television set. In that time, he will witness eighteen thousand dramatized murders. He will also become intimately acquainted with the sanguinary exploits of maniacal cops, blood-thirsty detectives, killer commandos, and sadistic criminals. His daily viewing fare will include killings, car crashes, knifings, rapes, fist fights, and torture.

And it's getting worse, not better. "Freddy's Nightmares," based on the Freddy Krueger character, which premiered last season, makes "Miami Vice" seem genteel by comparison.

In one episode, Adam, a high school senior, meets a mysterious woman (Lannic) at a party. She seduces him, but he awakes in the morning next to his girlfriend. A membrane connects them, which the girl proceeds to sever with a butcher knife. Blood spurts everywhere. In the next scene, Adam's father is being tortured by his mother. Lannic approaches Adam with a bloody blade. His girlfriend has been killed. He finds her head boiling in a pot on the stove.

In another episode, teen-aged Max is forced to work at his uncles' pizzeria. The latter has a "secret ingredient," which makes his pizzas very popular. Max unravels the mystery: his uncle has been murdering his friends and using their body parts as toppings (close-ups of bodies hanging in a meat locker, a finger going through a grinder). Max kills his uncle in revenge and uses him in the next batch. Freddy orders a "human" pizza and plucks out an eyeball which he pops into his mouth. Tasteful.

Dr. Leonard D. Efron, professor of psychology at the University of Illinois at Chicago, who studied the habits of more than four hundred viewers for twenty-two years, observes: "There can no longer be any doubt that heavy exposure to televised violence is one of the causes of aggressive behavior, crime and violence in society."

Adds Arnold Kahn of the American Psychological Association: "The debate over the effects of violence on television is like the debate over cigarette smoking and cancer."

There may not be a direct casual relationship. A six-year-old doesn't watch an episode of "Friday the 13th," grab a chain saw, and slice up Sis. Rather, the impact is cumulative. Weak personalities can be inclined toward violence by a regular blood-and-guts diet. Like the hero of action films, he comes to perceive the answer to all of life's little problems in a large caliber weapon.

Normal people also are affected. Televised slaughter is desensitizing. Watch enough of it, and you can't help but become less responsive to the very real suffering around you. Tens of thousands of hours viewing spectacles of death, with breaks for lite beer commercials, does not heighten feelings of compassion.

As a writer to the *Wall Street Journal* points out, the inanity of the switch-the-channel argument may be readily perceived by applying this rationale to other forms of pollution: Water pollution: Just don't drink the water. Air pollution: Don't breath the air. Trash in the streets: Don't use the streets.

Even assuming the channel-change argument is applicable to mature adults, many viewers are neither. Between the hours of ten and eleven, when this ocean of gore reaches its high-water mark, a quarter of all grade school children are still tuned in.

Like drug kingpins, TV executives are making a killing (literally as well as figuratively) marketing poison. It matters not into whose veins it flows, or its corrosive impact on our society, as long as the blood money keeps rolling in.

Hollywood sullies Jesus as symbol
(28 July 1988)

All that stands between America and rampant censorship, religious intolerance, nay theocracy itself is the vigilance of Universal Pictures. At least that is the implication of an ad the studio ran in the *New York Times* on July 21.

The advertisement was in response to critics of *The Last Temptation of Christ*, scheduled for release this fall. The blasphemous flick portrays Jesus as a paranoid, self-doubting, obsessive, guilt-ridden individual. Mary Magdalene, Jesus' ex-girlfriend in the film, is the object of his incessant fantasies. On the cross, there is a hallucinatory sequence in which he imagines that he's having intercourse with her, which—needless to say—is graphically portrayed.

It's hardly surprising that *Last Temptation*

depicts Christ as a psychotic degenerate. With Martin (*Taxi Driver*) Scorsese directing the movie, it's a wonder Jesus isn't shown mowing down the Temple moneychangers with an uzi.

Yet Christian leaders are understandably perturbed by the vile production. The Rev. Lloyd Ogilvie, of the First Presbyterian Church of Hollywood, calls it: "the most serious misuse of film craft in the history of filmmaking." Bill Bright, of the Campus Crusade for Christ, offered to reimburse the studio for the cost of production, if it would cancel the film.

It was to this proposal that Universal responded. "While we understand the deep feelings and convictions which have prompted this offer, we believe that to accept it would threaten the fundamental freedoms of religion and expression promised to all Americans under our Constitution," the studio self-righteously remarked.

After lecturing us on the dangers of "monolithic authorities" dictating "artistic expression and religious beliefs," the ad piously proclaimed that in America "no sect or coalition has the power to set boundaries around each person's freedom to explore religious and philosophical questions whether through speech, books or film." Take that, you Bible-banging, book-burning bigots!

Does freedom of expression require that every concept be explored; must every idea, no matter how bizarre and abhorrent, be articulated? Not merely expressed, but turned into a silver screen extravaganza? Is it essential to the furtherance of religious inquiry that Hollywood concoct a sex life for Jesus?

Reasonable limits, self-imposed, are not the same as censorship. The boundaries should be set by decency and sensitivity to the deeply held sentiments of our neighbors.

Contrast the salacious slander of *Last Temptation* to the respectful treatment of Islam in *Muhammad, Messenger of God*, produced a decade ago. In this dramatization, the prophet isn't shown on the screen or his voice heard by the audience, for fear of affronting devout Moslems. Though Islam does not consider Muhammad God incarnate, still this acute deference was afforded its founder.

Christians are the only group Hollywood can offend with impunity, the only creed it actually goes out of its way to insult. Clerics, from fundamentalist preachers to Catholic monks, are routinely represented as hypocrites, hucksters, sadists, and lechers. The tenets of Christianity are regularly held up to ridicule.

But why would Universal go to such a provocative extreme? Quite simply, because the entertainment industry has managed to degrade every other value: love, the family, patriotism. After nudity, gut-wrenching violence, simulated sex, and the display of every perversion catalogued in the annals of degeneracy, what is left for shock value?

Movie audiences have grown jaded with films which graphically present incest, fornication, sadomasochism, mutilation, and slaughter for their titillative effect. Hollywood must constantly seek new forms of exhibitionism, to stimulate box office sales.

In this competition of the sensational, Universal hit on a sure-fire winner: portray the man worshiped by 90 percent of the American people as a Judean Jimmy Swaggart. It isn't enough that Universal commit sacrilege in the pursuit of profits. While surrendering to the sweet temptation of Mammon, the studio insists on being congratulated for its fancied defense of the First Amendment.

Why stop at abusing Christians? Now that Hollywood has determined to enter the business of debunking sacred symbols, every faith can become a target for exploitation. Why not cinematic offerings showing Moses as a maniac, Muhammad as pedophile, Buddha doing drugs, and Krishna selling vinyl siding or engaging in some other loathsome activity?

As a Jew, I doubt I can be accused of sectarian bias in the controversy at hand. I do not believe in the divinity of Jesus Christ. I do believe in respecting the faith of those who regard him as their savior. Calls for Hollywood to exercise responsibility and a bit of charity are not the equivalent of censorship.

NINE

Drugs/Crime

Surrender won't work in war on drugs
(6 August 1992)

The solicitation from the Drug Policy Foundation did not bear a Colombian postmark. It did, however, typify the logic of the legalization crowd.

"Our government has spent nearly $100 billion in the last decade on a *harsh* drug war. [Are there other kinds of war?] Yet all of us are less safe. . . . While the drug war gets more money the rest of the economy suffers," the letter laments.

Blame for inner-city slaughter was laid at the door of "our failed drug policies." Unmet social needs and civil liberties alike are sacrificed on the high altar of drug prohibition.

Legalization advocates fancy that term—"prohibition"—analogizing current anti-drug efforts to the era of bootleg gin, another supposed failure to legislate abstinence. In a recent column, William F. Buckley, Jr., who bids us "Just Give Up," repeatedly used the expression *drug prohibition*.

On no subject do legalizers speak with greater assurance or more profound ignorance. Their mythology notwithstanding, Elliot Ness was not

151

involved in a trivial pursuit. The consumption of alcohol declined substantially during Prohibition. Between 1911 and 1929, the cirrhosis death rate for men was cut by two-thirds. Arrests for public drunkenness dropped 50 percent between 1916 and 1922. Prohibition ended when the American people decided that moderate imbibing was a vice we could live with, not because the law was unenforceable.

Like all utopians, legalizers conveniently ignore the historic record. We are told that legalization will lead to a dramatic drop in prices, providing less incentive to push drugs, hence less addiction.

That has not been the case in every society where drugs were sanctioned. According to Dr. Gabriel Nahas, a pharmacologist at Columbia University's College of Physicians and Surgeons, when Moslem societies removed restrictions on hashish in the sixteenth century: "A large number of people from all walks of life were in a constant state of intoxication."

In the mid-nineteenth century, Europe imposed the opium trade on China. By 1900 there were an estimated 90 million opium addicts in the nation. Opium use was finally suppressed through a Mandarin version of our "harsh drug war."

Recent legalization experiments are no more encouraging. During the years when British physicians could write prescriptions for heroin, the nation's junkies increased forty-fold.

Here's a snapshot of post-prohibition America, taken in the De Wallen district of Amsterdam, where Dutch authorities tolerate chemical euphoria. The *Los Angeles Times* reports: "Emaciated junkies slouch on the curbs, injecting themselves from syringes. . . . Heroin addicted prostitutes shiver in the doorways, beckoning customers with haunted, hollow eyes. Pill pushers, pimps and grungy dope runners clog the bridges."

As former Drug Policy Director William Bennett points out in his book, *The De-Valuing of America*, when inexpensive crack cocaine flooded this country in the early 1980s, the rate of addiction soared. Refuting the theory that cheap, legalized drugs would lead to a decline in crime (addicts won't have to steal to get it). Bennett says police and DEA agents told him that crime rates were the highest wherever drugs were cheapest.

But the price of legalization can't be calculated in dollars and cents alone. It's all well and good to speak of victimless crimes, to say that adults have a right to choose their own hell. But what about the others who are consigned to living torment, or violent death, along with them?

Drugs like cocaine tend to make users irrational, paranoid, violent. In New York City in 1987, 73 percent of child abuse cases involved parental drug use. The six-year-old beaten to death by an adult high on drugs will be just as dead if the drugs involved are legally obtained.

Is the drug war too expensive? We are spending $2.5 billion a year on intensive care for crack babies and billions more to educate them once they reach school age. If legalization resulted in a rise of addiction, as the historic experience suggests, what we save on law enforcement, we'll spend on medical care, shelters for battered women and children, and burial expenses.

The Drug Policy Foundation says drug war funding would be better spent on rehabilitation.

Wrong, on two important counts: 1) Most addicts
in treatment were forced into programs by the
criminal justice system. Legalize drugs and this
incentive disappears. 2) The rate of permanent
recovery is low. Every dollar spent on keeping
drugs out of the hands of kids (through interdic-
tion and punishment) is worth hundreds expended
on treatment later.

It was John Adams who noted that only a
moral people are capable of self-government. What
are the prospects for the survival of democracy in
a nation of addicts, in a society that declares that
losing one's soul is a matter of personal choice?

Needed: A moral crusade on drugs
(26 January 1989)

Of all George Bush's Cabinet-level appoin-
tees, drug czar William Bennett has perhaps the
hardest job but also the most superb qualifica-
tions to tackle the task.

As secretary of education, he argued passionately for returning an ethical perspective to learning. He urged a restoration of the classics for the
moral lessons they teach. While the surgeon general was busy extolling the virtues of condoms in
the fight against AIDS, Bennett's department issued an AIDS education handbook calling on parents and teachers to stress "appropriate moral
and social conduct" as the first line of defense
against the disease.

Sex education without values "is an evasion
and an irresponsibility," Bennett declared. One of
the most gratifying moments in his tenure as education chief, he disclosed, came during a visit to a
model school in the South Bronx. "I asked (a

class) why we studied Shakespeare, and a little boy got up and said, 'So we will learn the difference between bad character and good character.' . . . It was my epiphany."

In the work ahead, these convictions will stand him in good stead. Bennett now confronts a task as daunting as that of Winston Churchill on assuming command of the British nation during the darkest days of World War II.

In the present conflict, the body count has reached staggering proportions. An estimated 23 million Americans, one in ten, use an illicit drug at least once a month. (Six million are cocaine addicts.) Drug use is highest among the young. While only 6 percent of the over-twenty-five population use marijuana regularly, 22 percent of those ages eighteen to twenty-five smoke pot. Some 25 percent of high school students use illegal substances at least monthly.

Nor is drug use limited to the young and foolhardy or the dregs of society. A 1986 article in the *New England Journal of Medicine* reached the astounding conclusion that 40 percent of hospital physicians use drugs. In the same year, two-thirds of the applicants for the Fairfax County, Virginia, police force showed evidence of cocaine use.

Drugs are a major impetus to crime. According to the National Institute of Justice, nearly three-quarters of those arrested in the District of Columbia in 1986 tested positive for drugs (up from 50 percent in 1984). In New York City, drug use among criminals jumped from 42 percent in 1984 to 80 percent in 1986. The Bureau of Justice Statistics discloses that 20 percent of all murderers admit to being high when they committed their crime.

There's no shortage of proposed maneuvers to outflank the enemy. Liberals want more education, rehabilitation, and enforcement aimed at pushers. Conservatives favor a demandside approach, increasing the penalties on users.

Libertarians advocate legalization. The Rambo crowd would mobilize the armed forces to intercept the supply at our borders. Some of the proposals have merit, particularly the "zero-tolerance" program of prosecuting those in possession of any amount of illicit drugs. But none, either singly or in combination, addresses the underlying problem.

For those who contend the answer lies in increased funding, the results to date offer little encouragement. Federal spending on drug education and prevention rose from $117 million in fiscal 1981 to $454 million in fiscal 1988. Federal subsidies for rehabilitation programs grew from $205 million to $370 million in the same period. This dramatic expansion of federal involvement has paralleled the greatest rise in substance abuse in our history.

According to the experts, logistical support is having no discernible impact on the war. In a 1987 report, the National Institutes of Justice disclosed: "There is no consistent evidence that drug education programs either decrease or increase the likelihood that students will use drugs."

Rehabilitation? A Rand Corporation study of drug treatment programs in the nation's capital found: "Even those who initially succeed in treatment programs often slip back into drug use."

With every assault repulsed, it's time to open a second front, a values offensive. Our drug problem is essentially an ethical problem, another product of the moral crisis confronting our society. We are raising a generation without scruples—individuals who lack the fortitude to reject the pleasure principle.

For those who believe in nothing higher than the self, nothing more than this existence, what is the rationale for refusing any form of gratification? Most of us live with pain. Without ideals and inspiration, the urge to momentarily escape, via chemically-induced euphoria, can be overwhelming.

Our youth must be armed with an understanding of responsibility and a glimpse of eternity. It's one thing to tell a kid that drugs are bad for him and quite another to let him know that chemical corruption is evil, a sullying of the spirit endowed by his Creator.

What can a drug czar do in this regard? Not much and quite a bit. He can use his bully pulpit to advance a crucial thesis: that the best weapon in the anti-drug arsenal is character development.

Savagery of the human animal
(18 October 1987)

For the discerning, philosophical lessons frequently are found in the pages of daily newspapers. A recent incident in Saugus, Mass., illustrates the perilous state of humanity more forcefully than a dozen treatises by learned academicians.

On September 20, a seventh-grade lass was savagely beaten by two twelve-year-old girls. The incident started, as juvenile altercations so often do, with name calling followed by a challenge to fisticuffs.

What commenced in an ordinary way soon

took a nasty turn. One of the combatants put on rings to scar her opponent. The brass-knuckle pugilist was joined by an accomplice. Together they beat the other child to the ground, kicked her, jumped on her, and dragged her onto a cinder railroad track.

At this point, while the pigtailed brutes discussed plans to drown her in a nearby pond, the victim escaped, was rescued by a neighbor, and taken to a hospital for treatment.

She sustained a fractured cheek, broken nose, cracked rib, and countless cuts and bruises. Doctors initially feared her spleen was ruptured.

Local police were stunned by the brutality of this assault by junior high girls. What are we coming to when kids who should be playing with dolls instead seek diversion in customizing a classmate's face?

Which brings us (now the philosophy, please) to history's longest-running debate: What is man's nature? Modern liberalism is premised on the theory that mankind is inherently good, that basically benevolent individuals somehow are corrupted by political, economic, or social institutions.

Accepting the initial assumption, it logically follows that by reforming those institutions we will shortly reach utopia—a lion-and-lamb world devoid of violence, greed, poverty, loneliness, and other species of human suffering.

Liberals have strived to save perfectible man from his imperfect environment for the last two centuries. Socialism was advanced to banish the avarice thought to be endemic in free markets, humanism to sever the bonds of irrational faith and allow man's mind to lead him to happiness and sexual liberation to remove puritanical restraints and let our loving dispositions shine forth.

The twentieth century, which has hauled humanity through blood and slime (in the form of death camps, gulags, man-made famines, a crime explosion, and the utter debasement of human sexuality) should have dispelled such nonsensical notions.

All of the new systems and relationships have failed us miserably. Socialist states have devised methods of repression previously unimagined in the fevered fantasies of despots. Sexual license has resulted in the growth of exploitation, and the decline of spirituality has stimulated man's basest instincts.

The flaw, of course, is in the concept. Children, bless their sweet souls, are conclusive evidence of the same. If people are naturally noble, than kids—because they're closest to a state of nature (i.e., relatively unspoiled by tradition)—should be little angels.

Yet as any parent whose eyes are unclouded by sentiment can confirm, exactly the opposite is true. Essentially, children are unbridled appetite. On the whole they are greedy, inconsiderate, and terribly uncivilized. They are often cruel to the point of sadism, as anyone who has witnessed a mob of eight-year-olds mercilessly tormenting a weaker or mentally less-agile playmate will attest.

Children represent humanity in the raw. What comes easily isn't honesty, charity, and compassion, but callousness and lust. Conservatives—gosh, we're so smart—believe goodness must be taught, that decency must be inculcated (by education and example), a task requiring great diligence and enormous patience to overcome considerable resistance.

We believe legislative restraints, including morality legislation, are essential to keep the human beast in check, to prevent him from escaping his confines and rending his fellows.

In this regard, religion is essential. To live honorably, man must accept a moral code outside himself, not subject to revision or modification by human whim.

The animals are among us. Indeed, they are us. The great task of civilization is to tame our savage selves. If you doubt it, ask a certain adolescent girl who recently was stomped on by a pair of her cherubic peers, doing what comes naturally.

The rage builds in Middle America
(7 May 1992)

President Bush is in Los Angeles today. Governor Clinton was on hand earlier in the week. But neither the Squire of Kennebunkport nor the Rhodes scholar and veteran power player can begin to comprehend middle-class rage building over the L.A. riots.

Last week—when television news broadcasts showed us scenes of grinning looters running from stores, their arms laden with minor appliances—I had a call from an acquaintance, a middle-aged businessman of usually mild demeanor, who spent the first fifteen-seconds of the conversation shouting obscenities, so incensed was he by the anarchy. If Republicans had the brains and guts (dubious assumptions), they could mine a bonanza of votes from this mother lode of disaffection.

The Democrats are hopeless, having long ago mortgaged their souls to the civil rights establishment. Clinton, keen observer that he is, chided us for "not honestly confronting the problems of race and poverty," as if the decent, hardworking majority didn't face those problems every time we pay taxes to support a welfare mother and her illegitimate brood, or when we learn of the latest slaying of someone unfortunate enough to wander into the wrong neighborhood at night.

Mr. Bush symbolically surrendered when he met with civil rights hustlers while flames lit the L.A. skyline, letting *them* lecture *him* about racism in the American justice system.

Among the proposals he's expected to unveil today is a plan to allow HUD tenants to buy their apartments and tax breaks for businesses that set up shop in the war zone. (Any entrepreneur so imprudent as to go there after Watts and last week's orgy of destruction should build with asbestos.) Neither move will prevent the demagogues from inciting violence the next time they're upset by a verdict, nor will it stop street thugs (who admittedly have little interest in home ownership or employment) from turning their communities into infernos.

The middle class watches this spectacle in dumb amazement. Where are the expressions of concern for the casualties in the City of Angels? Where are the marches, the silent vigils for them? After all, Rodney King is still alive.

Where are the condemnations of the virulent racism played out in the street of our second largest city, with minority mobs attacking any whites or Asian-Americans they could lay their hands on? Of course, we realize that dragging a man from his truck and nearly beating him to death, for no other reason than the color of his skin, isn't a civil rights violation if the victim is Caucasian.

There's no prejudice in Middle America's reaction. We know that many of the victims are black. We saw brave black men running into the streets to snatch innocents from the jaws of a ravening beast.

But we are so very sick and tired of the Jesse Jacksons, the Benjamin Hooks, and the David Dinkins, the excuse-makers, the guilt-mongers, those who racialize every incident, whose incessant demands can never be satisfied.

While we're on the subject, we do not view the police as our enemies. The media sneeringly referred to the "thin blue line defense" in the King case. That's exactly the way most of us see it, a perception massively reinforced by last week's discount shopping spree.

Calls for more social spending to defuse racial tensions are drowned out by peals of derisive laughter. In constant dollars, total welfare expenditures soared from $156 billion in 1980 to $225 billion in 1990. Housing subsidies, food stamps health expenditures all increased dramatically—in real dollar terms—during the cruel Reagan-Bush years. If racial peace could be bought with welfare bribes, America's inner cities should be as serene as Bismarck, North Dakota, over a long Labor Day weekend.

Now they actually expect us to pay for the rebuilding of South Central L.A.—so they can incinerate it again the next time they feel like protesting racial injustice or the unequal distribution of Jack Daniels. Let the 9,500 arrested in the riots rehabilitate the area, brick by brick with their own hands, even if it takes a lifetime.

Slavery ended 130 years ago. Segregation has been a historical footnote for three decades. Quotas are a reality of life, with racial balancing overriding merit in nearly every field of endeavor. And still some insist on blaming every minority misfortune on white racism, while they sit in their public housing—nurtured on resentment and envy—whining for more hand-outs and indicting society for not giving them the businesses Koreans worked to acquire.

The media, which once again covered themselves with laurels here, are correct. There is racial injustice in America, though not the kind they imagine. There is an anger building in the suburbs, small towns, and ethnic neighborhoods which one day will be heard.

TEN

Pornography

The music that debases
(28 August 1985)

Sometimes a cultural disease can reach near epidemic proportions before it's even noticed. Fortunately, people are finally waking up to the porno-rock plague. A group of congressional wives, calling themselves the Parents Music Resource Center, have organized to combat this scourge.

PMRC advocates voluntary restraint by the recording industry, including a rating system similar to that used for movies, to alert parents to objectionable lyrics. To date, the industry has been somewhat less than responsive. Only records with the most offensive language have been tagged with a rather innocuous warning label ("Parental Guidance: Explicit Lyrics").

Recovering from the initial shock of a parental onslaught which caught them unawares, the music establishment has counter-attacked. Cries of censorship are heard from those who think the First Amendment is a heavy metal band.

Rock creature Frank Zappa interviewed on "Entertainment Tonight," declares he wants to put a sticker of his own on records, cautioning that those who object to obscene lyrics are witchhunters intent on destroying the Constitution. Zappa's views should be afforded the consideration due a man who would name his firstborn Moon Unit.

Parents are right to remonstrate against sleaze marketed as entertainment. Songs promoting drug abuse, promiscuity, perversion, suicide, rape, and murder saturate the airwaves.

This filth is purveyed by some of America's most popular recording artists. "Sugar Walls" (Sheena Easton) describes the pleasures of orgasm in graphic detail. "Eat Me Alive" (Judas Priest) concerns forced oral sex at gunpoint. Madonna moans it "feels so good inside" in "Like a Virgin." "Darling Nikki" (Prince) is a girl who performs an autoerotic act with a magazine. "Murder by the Numbers" (Rolling Stones) advocates the killing of family members.

Consider the inherent sadism of the punk rock ditties: "Let Me Put My Love Into You" ("Don't you struggle. Don't you fight; Let me put my love into you. Let me cut your cake with my knife.") "Live Wire" ("I'll either break her face or take down her legs. Get my ways at will. Go for the throat."), and "Whiplash" ("We are here to maim and kill 'cause this is what we choose.").

Are they just kidding? Is it all a put-on? Can an eleven-year-old tell the difference?

Look at the dead eyes staring out at you from album covers. Note that many rock legends (Janis Joplin, Jimi Hendrix) died of drug overdoses, more are addicts. Recall that punk rocker Sid Vicious murdered his girlfriend before destroying himself.

The morals of rockers are illustrated by the lovely Madonna, who commits sacrilege by wearing sacred symbols as ornaments and who posed nude before she started singing naked songs.

Those leading the assault on porn-rock maintain they like rock music *per se*. It's only the most bizarre manifestation of the genre they find objectionable.

I, on the other hand, have always loathed rock-and-roll. Some of it is barely acceptable (the Beatles song played by a symphony orchestra), tunes to listen to when you can't find a classical station on the car radio.

For the most part, rock bears only a passing resemblance to real music. It is blaring, discordant noise—the savage beat of the jungle, primal man shrieking his despair at a universe beyond his comprehension. Rock's chaotic sound naturally lends itself to the expression of primitive emotions.

Punk rock is the fruition of libidinous seeds sowed in the springtime of rock-and-roll. It isn't all that far from the pelvic gyrations of the genre's pioneers to the rocker who appears on stage adorned with a codpiece, a chainsaw blade dangling between his legs.

Rock is a symptom of a far deeper malady afflicting western civilization. Musicians who can barely spell the word philosophy would be incredulous on hearing that their songs reflect the sentiments of philosophers long dead.

Their lyrics are a call to spiritual anarchy, a rhythmic advertisement for nihilism. They proclaim the futility of existence—a life without purpose where salvation is found only in unrestrained sexual indulgence, rebellion, and violence.

The pseudo-sophisticates who claim no one was ever hurt by an idea must also believe no one was ever helped by the same. In fact, ideas can be deadlier than bullets.

Rock lyrics do indeed have an effect on listeners, particularly those lacking the discernment which comes with maturity. "You can't use a rhetoric for long without assuming the virtues and vices that lie behind it," says poet Tom Landess.

The words of popular songs, like other forms of artistic expression, can elevate or debase. They can clothe man in dignity and prompt him to aspire to nobility, or condone the expression of his basest passions. As rock increasingly fills the latter role, it should be shunned by civilized people.

2 Live Crew and the death of a nation
(25 October 1990)

You are witnessing the demise of a civilization—a slow death of a thousand cuts. Intellectuals (artists, critics, journalists, and jurists) forge the weapons the barbarians eagerly wield against us.

Two seemingly unrelated incidents last week are chapters of an unfolding tragedy. In Massachusetts, a thirty-two-year-old mother of three was convicted of sexually abusing her own children. The verses in Mother's Day cards weren't written for Terri Clements. During sex parties in her home, Clements would line up her sons against a wall and allow guests to pick their victim. If two wanted to use the same child, they would flip a coin to see who would go first. At the time, the youngest child was three, the oldest seven.

If music be the food of lust, a Broward County jury bids the band play on. Within days of Clements' conviction, a Florida court acquitted the rap group 2 Live Crew of obscenity charges. The middle-class jury found the group's charming ditties dripping with artistic merit, after experts like Henry Louis Gates, professor of literature at Duke University, testified that the lyrics were meant as a parody (an obscene parody?).

For the record, the group's album *Nasty As They Wanna Be*, is a string of obscenities set to music. The celebrated F-word is uttered 226 times. The word "bitch," used to address a woman commanded to gratify the singer's carnal cravings (oral, anal, or vaginal), is used 163 times. Explicit terms for male or female genitalia are employed 117 times, while there are no fewer than 87 descriptions of oral sex. The rap group is to music what toilet-stall graffiti is to literature.

The Crew trial called to mind the recently concluded Cincinnati case, where a jury determined the scatological/sadomasochistic work of Robert Mapplethorpe was not obscene. In interviews after the verdict, jurors made it clear that they really wanted to convict. But what could we do, they pleaded, with all of these experts—museum curators, art historians, critics—telling us it's art.

This is the ultimate tyranny of the authorities—day is night, up is down, if a few academic idiots, credentialed cretins, testify to the same. I'm sure I could locate a passel of Ph.D.s to attest to the cinematic artistry of *Debbie Does Dallas* ("The witty and sophisticated response of a young woman to Southwestern culture." "A parody of the cowboy genre of filmmaking.")

While we congratulate ourselves on our tolerance of diversity, the screams of women and children echo around us. There is a connection between pornography sanctified as art and a rising tide of victimization that consists of creating a climate conducive to sexual aggression.

Want an expert opinion or two? Janet Kardon, the original curator to the Mapplethorpe collection, observes that all of the photographer's nudes, including children, were meant to be erotic. Also: "Looking is typically the first step in sexual arousal." Jed Perl, art critic for the decidedly leftist *Partisan Review*, says Mapplethorpe "made a conscious decision for obscenity" and "upped the ante" when he photographed a sad-faced little girl with her dress raised to expose her genitals.

Judith Reisman, author of a Justice Department report on the exploitation of children in mainstream skin magazines and the only expert to testify for the prosecution in the Cincinnati case, notes there is never an extraneous element in Mapplethorpe's works.

In "Jesse McBride," we see a little boy posed naked on top of a chair with an electrical cord coming into the picture at an angle. What is the message here, in light of the fact that these cords are among the most commonly used instruments in the physical and sexual torture of children? Mapplethorpe's kiddie porn is particularly ominous when displayed with other photos which extol violence, degradation, and perversion.

Mapplethorpe's works legitimize pedophilia. Crew's songs celebrate sexual rage. (The creatures convicted in August of the brutal gang rape of a Central Park jogger last year hummed rap tunes at their arraignment.) That this visual/auditory incitement can be shown in museums, played in concerts, funded with tax dollars (As a reward for its diligence, Congress has decided to increase the NEA's appropriation by $9 million for the current cycle and remove any meaningful restraints on its funding of obscenity.) is society's way of saying it's quite acceptable.

Can it be long before this art is displayed in public schools?

How can we object to more plebeian porn (the sort sold in adult bookstores) when the chic variety is celebrated in exhibits and sexual savages strut their smut before thousands of concertgoers?

Welcome to a nation where the immature bodies of children are perverts' playthings, a society where women can't walk safely down urban streets. A country gets the culture it deserves. Ours is dying. Intellectuals are doing the embalming. The poor, dumb, intimidated middle class is funding the funeral.

The sleaze factor
(10 July 1985)

This is not a movie review. Having made that disclaimer, I must confess that the new Steven Spielberg film, *Goonies*, is marvelous in every way save one. Yet the film's only flaw is so significant that parents with young children should avoid it like the plague.

Goonies is vintage Speilberg, and that's heady stuff for devotees of action films. There are enough menacing villains, scary chases, close escapes, and Rube-Goldberg type booby traps (not to mention the waterslides, pirate ships, and hidden treasure) to satisfy the most avid Indiana Jones fan. This is clearly a children's summer movie. The central characters are all pre-teens. Its action sequences will have particular appeal for the young, making it all the more pernicious.

The film's moral Achilles' heel is its vulgar language—a dump-truck dirt load of the stuff. Especially at the outset of the movie, these kids talk trash. The dialogue is peppered with vulgar expressions for copulation, genitalia, and excrement—the ubiquitous F-, S-, and C-words. It was particularly disturbing to hear barroom expressions bandied about by fresh-faced kids. Summertime, and the movies are sleazy.

The make-your-peace-with-the-world-you-live-in side of me says: So what? Don't be an old fogey. That's the way kids talk today. Compared to the other things seen or heard in the cinema (nudity, graphic violence, the depiction of every conceivable perversion—and many which are barely imagined), four-letter words are a matter of little consequence.

To this my saner side rejoins: Be a fogey; this is something you should care deeply about. Corruption begins with ideas, conveyed by words. (See the serpent enticing us with a tasty bit of fruit.) First the utterance, then the act. The slippery slide to life's sewer starts with offhand expressions.

Once we had a sense of propriety. Now, profanity abounds in what passes for culture in these United States. Gutter words for male and female reproductive organs, snickering references to the sexual act, and scatological terminology are the common coin of expression for everyone from construction workers to college professors.

There's hardly a movie made today, unless it's set in a nineteenth century convent, without scads of dirty words. Tough-talking cops, wise-cracking kids, teens with excessive libidos, even mild-mannered suburbanites let loose torrents of obscenity at the least provocation—a volcano of vulgarity.

Vulgarity is supposed to lend an air of reality to the cinema. Isn't this the way people actually converse? Yes, but their vocabulary is at least in part a reflection of Hollywood's tutelage, a case of movies and TV expanding the boundaries of acceptability to the outer limits of bad taste.

It's hard to escape the obscenity barrage. Much of the most objectionable movie dialogue wends its way into American homes each evening, via cable television, to corrupt the innocent. Who is so naive as to believe that only adults watch the 8 P.M. movie on Home Box Office?

Popular fiction, which bears absolutely no relationship to literature, reinforces the trend. Studds Lonigan was refined—a gentleman of the old school—compared to the characters in an Erica Jong novel.

Comics plumb the depths of the cesspool for humor. T-shirts, besides advertising such intimate details as the absence of virginity, often broadcast the wearer's sentiments on a variety of subjects in toilet terms.

Society sinks to the lowest common denominator. As soon as profanity was popularized in the cultural medium it wasn't long before obscenities were slithering into everyday parlance. As a result, we are fast becoming a verbal sewer society. Adults demonstrate their pseudo-sophistication by spouting four-letter words. Teens are caught up in the obscenity chic. Children ape their elders. One of the saddest spectacles on earth is a twelve-year-old girl with a truck driver's vocabulary.

You are what you speak. Vulgarity has a coarsening effect. Speech should elevate our thoughts; obscenity depresses them.

Constantly describing sex in aggressive, gutter terms debases the concept. If young people develop a casual attitude toward coitus (leading to burgeoning teen pregnancy, abortion, and sex outside marriage), is it any wonder? Victorians spoke of love in almost lyrical terms; we feel compelled to use barnyard expressions to convey romantic notions. I ask you, who has the hang-ups?

Relating everyday activities to the process of elimination sets us back to the communication level of infants with a fecal fascination. Our ideas become as disposable as that which exits through sanitary drain pipes.

The dignity of man is ill served by a vocabulary that reduces the human experience to the bedroom and the bathroom.

ELEVEN

Abortion/Euthanasia

Life scores a win in Washington
(7 November 1991)

Washington state narrowly eluded a societal death when voters rejected a ballot question which would have made their state the first jurisdiction anywhere in the world to legalize what is euphemistically termed "assisted suicide." Medical murder is a more apt description.

Had the initiative passed, on the certification of two physicians that he had less than six months to live, a patient could have enlisted the aid of his doctor in ending his life.

A slight problem would have complicated the process. Medical science, being finite in its wisdom, often miscalculates. An ad by opponents of the initiative featured a man who was told he had two weeks to live. That was four years ago.

The good death, they call it. Why endure a protracted, fatal ailment when we can slip quietly into oblivion? The desire to alleviate pain, our own or that of a loved one, is among the most natural of emotions. When compassion clouds our judgement, it's also among the most dangerous.

Once the syringe-bearing genie is out of the bottle, who can say what homicidal wonders he may next perform?

Patients can rationally decide to end their life, it is asserted. But how rational is the person who has just learned he's about to die? Once suicide is sanctioned, the burden will be on the dying to justify their continued existence. How many will choose a quick death not because that is their natural inclination, but out of a sense of obligation—to spare their family a financial or psychological burden?

It's a short step from complying with the wish of a dying patient to making the decision for him. While assisted suicide isn't legal in the Netherlands, it is tolerated. A study commissioned by the Dutch government disclosed that in 1990, 1,030 patients were killed without their consent (in other words, murdered). Of these, 140 were fully competent and 110 only mildly mentally impaired.

Substantial resources go toward extending the lives of the elderly, who may have but a few years to live. What is the quality of life of an eighty-year-old, semi-invalid living in a nursing home, compared to the cost of maintaining that existence? How great will be the temptation to help them, with or without their permission, to a dignified demise. Understandably, 90 percent of Dutch nursing home patients oppose euthanasia.

If there is a right-to-die, how can it rationally be restricted to the terminally-ill? Why withhold the boon from those whose illness, while not fatal, is painful, debilitating, and so significantly diminishes the caliber of life as to make death an attractive alternative? Of the two women recently escorted to the pearly gates by Dr. Jack Kevorkian, neither was even close to death. One had multiple sclerosis, the other a painful pelvic disease.

And how can we deny a merciful death to the chronically depressed? As anyone who has worked in the mental health field knows, there is psychic suffering which rivals the most acute physical pain. Again, if it is your life—and yours alone—how can your "right" to dispose of the same logically be limited to a terminal condition?

Let us leave the slippery slope, realistic as it is, and return to the matter at hand. Consider the case of the person in pain, lingering at death's doorstep. Is it not barbaric to consign him to weeks or months of agony?

In an increasingly secular age, it's difficult to explain the value of suffering. The very notion of good coming out of evil seems monstrous, downright un-American. Most of us order our lives on the principle of pain avoidance.

We look at the man or woman dying in a hospital bed and ask how their life—what little they have left of it—could possibly have meaning. But who, other than the bard, can get beneath another's skin or peer into his soul? Even in recollections, remembrance, there can be joy. Some only experience ultimate clarity in the process of a natural death. Which is why, at some point, most of the dying become reconciled to their mortality.

The dying can still love and be loved, which—after all—is the most human act, the pinnacle of existence. In an age when heroes are in terribly short supply, our capacity to endure pain with dignity can serve as an inspiration to survivors.

The above is speculation. Ultimately, the value of death, like the value of life, is a mystery known only to the author of human destiny. Is there a right to die? But our life wasn't self-generating. Where is the right to discard that which was given by another? As Rabbi David Bleich, professor of Talmud and ethics at Yeshiva University, puts it: "Autonomy does not extend to one's own life. Man's body and life are the property of the Creator."

The Washington state vote is the opening salvo in what promises to be a protracted engagement. The pandora's box of euthanasia is an open grave. Unless we begin thinking—not emotionally, but critically—the Judeo-Christian ethic could be interred therein.

Abortion advocates threaten again . . .
(27 January 1992)

Every time I decide to stop writing about abortion, the other side makes one of its famous, logic-defying declarations that gets me going again.

So the U.S. Supreme Court will rule on the constitutionality of the Pennsylvania abortion law, another anticipated blow to—a little trumpet voluntary for dramatic effect here—a woman's right to choose. *Roe vs. Wade* is supposed to have the same life expectancy as a fetus in a Planned Parenthood clinic.

Once again the National Abortion Rights Action League, National Organization for Women, etc. are issuing their everybody-tremble-and-lose-bladder-control warnings: If the high court upholds Pennsylvania's restrictions, there will be electoral hell to pay.

Zillions of women who've never voted single-issue before will rise up and smite the forces of reproductive oppression. No, this time we're not kidding—they insist—unlike the last three presidential campaigns and most statewide races since the *Webster* decision.

But back to the braying of the booboisie. "The voters will remember in November," chimed U.S. Sen. Tom Harkin (D-Iowa), sounding every bit the corn-fed Jesse Jackson. They'll recall that "George Bush endorsed and presided over the loss of a fundamental, constitutional, established right for all women in the country."

Democratic presidential candidates are expected to make utter fools of themselves to appease their gyno-terrorist allies. But let's be at least marginally real. When the Supreme Court at last addresses *Roe* directly, it will not be to deny a "fundamental, constitutional, established right" to abortion. Such a right never was.

For 184 years from the adoption of the Constitution—rather a lengthy gestation period—no one knew that it contained abortion rights. The Founding Fathers were blissfully ignorant of their existence. It wasn't until 1973, following a decade of capricious jurisprudence, that those intrepid ideological explorers, Harry Blackmun and William Brennan, in delving the darkest recesses of the First Amendment's penumbra, discovered the right to dispose of inconvenient life. It took justices obsessed with population control, who had raised anarchic autonomy to holy writ, to fabricate the pseudo-right.

What gross injustice has the state of Pennsylvania wrought? Mandating a twenty-four-hour waiting period for a life-or-death decision? Spousal notification, based on the incredible assumption that a father might have some interest in the survival of his child? Informed consent—requiring a doctor to advise a woman of the age of her unborn child and offer to provide her with literature explaining stages of fetal development and enumerating alternatives to abortion?

It's not as if the physician in question will get the mother in a half-nelson and force her to read right-to-life pamphlets. The same people who shriek "choice" with the least provocation, who (on the question of Title X funding) rage about keeping women in the dark, would deliberately deny them the data for an intelligent decision.

What do you say to someone who prattles about the "right to choose," but obstinately refuses to consider the *object* of that choice, which—it so happens—is a living human being, with (after the eighth week of gestation) a complete genetic code, heartbeat, brain waves, limbs, and all vital organs?

How do you make them understand that a right requires a moral foundation? That in two thousand years of Western civilization, there has never been a recognized right to absolute control of one's body (to take heroin, for instance, or commit suicide)? That we are cannibalizing our children, uprooting future generations for current lifestyle consumption? That in order to avoid confronting the ugly reality of this choice, we pretend that the life within is only a lump of protoplasm?

How do you get them to think about the long-term implications of the abortion ethos, of the mortal storm we've unleashed? Spina bifida babies are starved to death. Feeding tubes are removed from comatose patients. Washington state barely escaped legalized suicide. A former governor says the elderly ill have a duty to die. Once society or its designated surrogates has the power to eliminate inconvenient life, where do we stop?

One of Dear Abby's readers anxiously inquires as to the advisability of throwing rice at a wedding. She's heard it expands in the tummies of birds, wounding the warblers. We're all for the birds. Ditto whales, seals, dolphins, spotted owls, stray cats—you name it. Will we show even a smidgen of concern for the endangered people (who are slaughtered at the rate of 1.5 million a year)? Stay tuned to Supreme Court dicta and election results for the answer.

Planned Parenthood's hidden agenda
(2 March 1989)

You'd think the Planned Parenthood Federation of America would blush to speak of the hidden agenda of its adversaries. But then, candor and consistency have never been its strong suit.

The cavaliers of contraception have launched another media blitz, aimed at selling their program to an administration whose existence they ardently opposed in the last election. The campaign's theme is: "A Kinder, Gentler America Begins With Family Planning" (but not for a million and a half unborn children a year, for whom Planned Parenthood's brand of kindness in the pursuit of family limitation consists of a curette or suction device).

Each ad is more illogical and offensive than the last. But one in particular caught my eye. In a national news magazine, the group ran a full-page polemic featuring a photo of a maniacal-looking gent, screaming into a loudspeaker: "I don't think Christians should use birth control."

The ad copy alerts us: "Leading 'pro-lifers' are usually careful to avoid condemning birth control in public. Yet they lobby behind the scenes, and have already succeeded in shaping federal policy and limiting family planning assistance."

The "family planning assistance" right-to-lifers oppose involves public funding of clinics that perform or promote abortion. Because Planned Parenthood views the lethal procedure as just another form of birth control, it naturally assumes that objection to abortion is opposition to contraception.

In alleging covert causes, Planned Parenthood is treading on perilously thin ice. From its founding, the organization has always had its own clandestine platform discreetly shielded from the general public behind a facade of mom, apple pie, and the intrauterine device—a program including radical feminism, sexual liberation, and population control.

Margaret Sanger, Planned Parenthood's founder and patron saint (referred to by Faye Wattleton, current national president, as "our courageous and outrageous leader"), was far more open than her successors. An advocate of what her era termed "free love", Sanger denounced monogamous marriage as a "degenerate institution" and touted "voluntary associations" between sexual partners.

She viewed motherhood as the enslavement of her gender. Birth control and abortion were intended to liberate womankind from this biological servitude. In 1914, in her periodical *Woman Rebel*, Sanger set forth her feminist credo—a woman's right "to live, to love, to be lazy, to be an unwed mother, to create, *to destroy*."

Initially a socialist ("I look forward to seeing humanity free someday of the tyranny of Christianity no less than capitalism"), late in life Sanger became a convert to racial eugenics. In this period, her favorite slogans were "More children for the fit, fewer for the unfit" (the latter encompassing all non-Nordics) and "Birth control to breed a race of thoroughbreds." The April 1933 issue of Sanger's *Birth Control Review*, devoted entirely to eugenics, included an article by Dr. Ernst Rudin, a leader of Hitler's forced sterilization/euthanasia program.

How closely does Planned Parenthood adhere to the ideology of its founder? Its attitude toward sex at least condones, some would say encourages, promiscuity.

"We think there is nothing wrong with sex . . . choose the sex life you want," beams Sol Gordon in a PPFA pamphlet.

"If, however, you have separated your sex and love needs," Harvey Kaplan, M.D., then a staff clinician at Planned Parenthood-World Population, helpfully observed, "then you could have a hundred partners and still be a perfect candidate for a good close relationship later on. So having multiple sexual partners in itself doesn't mean anything."

While sex is good, an end in itself, in what Planned Parenthood perceives to be a critically overcrowded, ecologically imbalanced world, children are viewed as a contagion. Sexologist Mary Calderone, former PPFA medical director, bemoans the fact that: "We are still unable to put babies in the class of a dangerous epidemic, even though that is the exact truth."

In 1969, then PPFA President Alan Guttmacher foresaw the "possibility that eventually coercion may become necessary" in the population control crusade, particularly "in areas where the pressure is greatest, possibly in India and China." Not surprisingly the regulators of reproduction have nothing but praise for the People's Republic, whose kindness includes forced third-trimester abortions.

Like the mother of their movement, Planned Parenthood views abortion as the key to realizing the feminist millennium. Women are disadvantaged from birth by the ability to conceive. Only by offering free and unrestricted access to abortion can "real equality between the sexes" be achieved. A revealing 1985 PPFA ad in *Ms. Magazine* has a woman insisting "the right to choose abortion makes all my other rights possible."

As it pockets our tax dollars and lectures us about benevolence and compassion, this is the covert course charted by Planned Parenthood. I can hardly wait for the first ad explaining this agenda to the American people.

Parents in the dark on abortion
(11 December 1989)

Who's best qualified to counsel a pregnant teen on the physical and psychological consequences of aborting her unborn child: A) the boyfriend who impregnated her, B) her fifteen-year-old, MTV-addicted girlfriend, C) the counselor at the local abortion clinic, which stands to make a tidy, taxpayer-funded profit from the procedure, or D) the people who gave her life and have cared for her since birth?

Oh, definitely not the last, cry the champions of choice, who fret that the Supreme Court might sanction parental notification laws in a pending case. Why it's a flagrant violation of reproductive rights, the abortion lobby laments.

Fortunately, the public does not share this warped perspective. A recent poll, reported in *USA Today*, discloses that 75 percent "believe that parents should be notified before their daughter under the age of 18 has an abortion." A *Detroit News* survey indicates Michigan residents support a parental consent bill, a considerably more stringent measure, passed by the legislature last week, by a 3-to-1 margin.

One is struck by the Mad Hatter quality of the current situation. In most states, a teen-ager needs her parents' written permission to get aspirin from the school nurse. But the same minor can waltz into an abortion clinic and submit to a potentially hazardous operation without so much as a by-your-leave to Mom and Dad.

Despite the claims of its proponents, abortion isn't the medical equivalent of having your hair styled. A Canadian study of 84,000 teen-aged abortions disclosed a high rate of complications: laceration of the cervix (12 percent), hemorrhage (8 percent), infections (7 percent), and a perforated uterus (4 percent).

One of those joining in an amicus brief in the Supreme Court case is Rachel Ely. At seventeen, Ely had an abortion arranged by her high school guidance counselor. Several days later, she experienced flu-like symptoms in her chest. Because there was no discomfort in the pelvic area, Ely assumed it wasn't related to the abortion.

In fact, she had developed bacterial endocarditis from a post-abortion surgical infection. This resulted in a blood clot, which became lodged in her brain, causing a stroke. Today Ely is in a wheelchair. Had her parents been aware of the operation they might have made the connection between the symptoms and her abortion. Timely treatment with antibiotics could have averted the tragedy.

Abortion advocates argue that parental disclosure might lead to undue pressure on teens, as if such decisions are made in a vacuum. In another study, 78 percent of teen-agers who aborted said they'd been strongly influenced by someone (a boyfriend, clinic personnel) who urged the procedure.

In a letter to U.S. Sen. Gordon Humphrey, Sue Liljenbert, who had an abortion at seventeen, related the following: "When I questioned the development of my baby, I was told (by a clinic staffer) that it wasn't a baby yet, and that it looked like a tadpole. . . . I had no scientific facts that day, only biased opinions. I was not told what abortion itself could do to me in the years to come, only that it was 'safe and simple.'

"I was not told that I would abuse myself with alcohol, try to kill myself, develop an eating disorder, and have terrible dreams. Worst of all, I was not told that I might never have another child. It has been fourteen years since my 'safe and simple' abortion, and I will never be able to have another child."

With notification, parents have the opportunity to deal with the underlying problem (peer pressure, exploitation, ignorance) which led to the pregnancy. At the very least, they could make doctors aware of their daughter's medical history, limiting the possibility of complications.

The same forces opposed to parental involvement, the Planned Parenthood/good sex gang, created the teen pregnancy crisis: by instructing pubescent boys and girls that sex of any sort is wholesome, and should be indulged in with gusto; by teaching the mechanics of sex, divorced from morality; by offering birth control and abortion as the easy answer to the adolescent passions they've incited.

How can we complain about the decline of the family if we countenance a system in which parents are deliberately kept in the dark about a matter which involves a high risk of harm to their children?

Fetal rights lose a few rounds
(29 April 1991)

A society doesn't arrive at Auschwitz overnight. There are always perilous portents—laws, judicial decisions, popular prejudices—which should sound an alarm in the minds of all but the most impervious.

Those warning bells resound like temple gongs across America. The highest court in Michigan recently dismissed the case of a woman charged with delivering cocaine to her unborn child on the grounds that what a woman does with *or to* her gestating child is nobody's business but her own.

A similar ruling was rendered by the Plymouth, Mass., Superior Court last week "Because of the intrusion required by this prosecution; namely the state's attempt to reach and deter be-

havior during pregnancy . . . [the defendant's]
privacy rights are seriously threatened," the court
held. Thus, the privacy doctrine evolves from a
rationale for abortion to an excuse for child abuse.

Giving your kid a habit is far from trivial. We
can only guess at the torment of a newborn junkie.
We do know that many find even a gentle touch
excruciatingly painful. The trauma continues
throughout their lives, with severe learning dis-
abilities and emotional disorders.

But none of that matters in pro-choice dogma,
because the child wasn't a person when the drugs
were administered. While it may be a person who
suffers today, at the time the damage was done
the victim was "part of the mother's body." How
can you victimize a lump of protoplasm?

Yes, I know all about the dreaded fetal police
and feminist fantasies of pregnant women forced
to take vitamins. Perhaps we should abolish child
abuse laws, for fear the cops will arrest parents for
sending Bobby to bed without dinner.

Pro-choicers live in mortal fear of any recognition of the humanity of the unborn. In 1989,
feminists were up in arms over another Massachusetts case. At the time, the Middlesex County district attorney tried to prosecute a woman for the
motor vehicle death of her unborn child. The
woman, later convicted of driving while intoxi-
cated with a revoked license, delivered a baby in
its ninth month stillborn, after wrapping her car
around a telephone pole.

The ACLU, NOW, and Planned Parenthood
all intervened in the defendant's behalf. It didn't
matter that the child was viable. At the time of the
accident, it had yet to pass through the birth ca-

nal, a journey which magically confers personhood on what was formerly a nonentity.

This bizarre, albeit consistent, ideology is evident in the debate over the medical use of fetal tissue. The week of the Michigan decision, ardently pro-abortion U.S. Rep. Henry Waxman (D-California) held hearings to overturn the ban on the use of federal funds in fetal transplant therapy.

Tissue and organs harvested from the tiny victims of abortion may be used to treat a number of neurological disorders. Why waste all of this prime flesh (from 1.5 million annual abortions), medical ghouls eagerly inquire? Many would go further. If we can use fetal cadavers, why not also exploit the tissue of live, nonviable fetuses, some scientists ask?

If it's moral to use the body parts obtained as a by-product of abortion, why not allow a woman to conceive and carry a child for the express purpose of aborting to obtain its tissue, suggests John Robertson, a law professor at the University of Texas? Several years ago, a woman sought to be inseminated with her father's sperm so she could cultivate new kidney tissue for him.

Someday the technology will exist to keep aborted fetuses alive in the laboratory, so their tissue can be collected not once but periodically and at the peak of freshness. A nightmarish vision no doubt, but other than the offense to one's sensibilities, how can proponents of fetal non-personhood conceivably oppose it?

As an *amicus* brief in the Webster case pointed out, a non-person has no rights. He or she "is no better off than property, entirely subject to the whim of the owner." If the fetus isn't human—the underlying premise of *Roe v. Wade*—we can kill it, experiment with it (pharmaceutical firms have conducted in utero experiments), use its corpse for spare parts, and inflict life-long and irreparable damage on the individual it will inevitably become by drug and alcohol abuse.

The Nazis, too, experimented on victims whose humanity they denied, utilized their remains to benefit the living. You're offended by that analogy? Sorry, the parallels are just too sickeningly ominous to ignore.

Therefore Choose Life: Judaism and Abortion

(Speech delivered at Dartmouth College, 12 November 1991)

They tell us abortion will play a prominent role in the 1992 campaign. If so, it will merely be the latest chapter in an exceedingly long work in progress.

For almost twenty years, America has been a nation at war with itself, embroiled in a debate whose roots reach to our deepest understanding of the nature of human life, the rights of the individual and the responsibilities of society.

Like most disagreements about fundamental issues, the dialogue is often acrimonious. Each side attempts to secure the moral high ground and rain righteous indignation upon the opposition's advancing forces. One side shouts "freedom," "equality," "individual rights;" the other counters with cries of "sanctity of life," "compassion," and "justice." As the battle is joined in legislatures, in courts, on editorial pages, and at polling places across the country, neither side seems inclined to give much ground.

Can Judaism make a contribution to the debate? Does Jewish teaching on this controversial subject hold any relevance for the gentile world, in other words for the 97 percent of America that's not Jewish?

Unquestionably. Judaism is the moral foundation of all Western religion. Those social issues most hotly disputed in America of the 1990s were first addressed near the dawn of recorded time by the patriarchs and prophets. In the words of Ecclesiastes, there is no new thing under the sun. Their wisdom can light our way in these increasingly benighted times.

Judaism has always been deeply concerned with questions of right and wrong. Justice, justice shalt thou pursue, the Torah commands.

About 3,300 years ago, a group of nomadic shepherds came out of the desert and onto the stage of history with a revolutionary message. Among the smallest of nations, they have had the most profound effect on Western civilization. Jews came into a blood-drenched, pagan world (one that worshipped might and glorified violence) with a life-transforming doctrine: that there is but one God—the Eternal, the Creator of life, ruler of the universe, and author of human destiny—and that our Maker and Master has two basic demands of us: righteousness and holiness.

In Judaism, morality isn't relative, neither are ethics situational. Right and wrong are based not on the outcome of opinion surveys, referenda, elections, or court cases, but on eternal, superhuman standards. As a Catholic theologian once noted: "It is good to recall that at Mount Sinai God gave the Jews the Ten Commandments, not the Ten Suggestions."

As Lord Immanuel Jakobovits, former Chief Rabbi of the United Kingdom, explains, Judaism "insists that the norms of moral conduct can be governed neither by the accepted notions of public opinion nor by the individual conscience. In the Jewish view, the human conscience is meant to enforce laws, not to make them."

Judaism was the first religion to oppose human sacrifice. The first to punish murder, regardless of the murderer's social status or the condition of his victim, the first to demand one standard of justice for all—the lowly no less than the high born, the widow and orphan as well as the warrior and king. The idea that we are all equal in the eyes of God (equal in our rights and responsibilities)—so eloquently articulated in the Declaration of Independence—originated in the Hebrew Scriptures.

Judaism has always been committed to the defense of life. It's not that we believe that this earthly existence is all there is, that life is an end in itself, but that life is a precious gift from God, whose preservation is our solemn duty.

You might say that Judaism, unlike some religions of the Far East, is a life-affirming faith. The God of Israel is referred to as the God of Life (to distinguish him from the deities of the ancient world, who were literally as well as figuratively, gods of death). His law is called *Torah Chayim*, the Torah of Life. On Rosh Ha-Shana, the Jewish New Year, Jews greet each other with *Le-Shana*

Tova teekataivu, "May you be inscribed (in the Book of Life) for a good year." The classic Jewish toast is *L'chayim*—"To life," an appropriate wish for a people whose very existence (spiritual as well as physical) has been constantly threatened throughout two millennia of exile.

A reverence for life suffuses Jewish law. Judaism was the first religion to prohibit cruelty to animals. Even the so-called ritual aspects of Judaism are steeped in ethical significance. Our dietary laws are essentially a moral code. To be kosher, an animal must be slaughtered in the most humane manner, to assure the least degree of suffering. (Indeed, it has been said, not without justification, that vegetarianism is the Jewish ideal.) By not eating milk and meat together, we symbolically separate life and death; milk (the source of nourishment for the young of mammals) representing life, meat symbolizing death.

This regard for life even extends to its lowliest forms. Thus Judaism prohibits the gratuitous destruction of trees.

Besides a reverence for life, Judaism is preoccupied with obligations. *Halacha* (Jewish law) spells out, in the most minute detail, our responsibilities toward parents, spouses, children, strangers, the poor, employees, employers, customers, our community, and nation.

It would be surprising, therefore, if Judaism had nothing to say about the most hotly contested moral issue of our times, one which is literally a matter of life or death, and has the potential to demolish that moral code, known as the Judeo-Christian ethic, on which our civilization rests.

Jewish law isn't explicit on the subject of elective abortion for a very simple reason: from biblical times until quite recently, the practice was nearly nonexistent in Jewish communities. Jews who were virtually alone in the ancient world in rejecting infanticide and euthanasia (an attitude the ancient Greeks considered a barbaric prejudice) opposed the casual destruction of life at any stage.

What is the status of the fetus in Jewish law? Is it considered a human being, nascent humanity, or nothing at all? Does it have the same rights as postnatal life, some rights, or no rights?

In the abortion debate, the most distorted biblical injunction appears in Exodus 21:22-23. Here Mosaic law holds that if two men are fighting and accidentally injure a pregnant woman so that she miscarries, her husband shall receive only monetary damages. Since the death penalty, which is mandated for the taking of a *nefesh* or human life, is not invoked in this case, proponents of abortion (Jewish and Christian) reason that the unborn child is not considered a person.

This is, to say the least, disingenuous. It's not an either-or situation. Because an unborn child doesn't have the same *halachic* standing as postnatal life, does not mean that it counts for nothing.

Judaism regards the unborn child as potential or developing life, certainly more than mere tissue, or a collection of cells. Thus the verse in Exodus mentioned above refers to the fetus as *Y'ladehah*—her children.

Various Jewish commentators describe the unborn child as "germinating life," "human life on the way," "possessing a human dimension."

The Book of Job (31:15) asks: "Did not He who made me in the womb make him? Did not the same one fashion us before our birth?" Isaiah (44:24) reads: "Thus says the Lord, your Redeemer, Who formed you in the womb, I am the Lord, Who made all things." And again in Jeremiah (1:4,5): "The word of the Lord came to me thus: Before I formed you in the womb I dedicated you. . . ." Talmudic literature speaks of the fetus in its mother's body joining in praise of the Almighty, while the Zohar (the classic work of Jewish mysticism) calls the fetus "the handiwork of the Living God."

A recognition of the humanity of the unborn child permeates Jewish law. The Sabbath, the most sacred day of the Jewish calendar, can only be violated when human life is at stake. Yet from biblical times, the Sabbath could be broken to save a fetus.

In his article "A Talmudic Overview of Abortion," Rabbi Aryeh Spero notes: "It was the practice of the Sanhedrin not to bring to trial a pregnant woman accused of a capital offense until after her delivery. Since the fetus, as the rabbis reasoned, is a form of life, they delayed her trial so that if a guilty verdict was rendered, the innocent fetus would not be killed."

Jewish priests (*Kohanim*), who served in the Holy Temple, were not allowed to touch, or even come in close proximity to, a human corpse. Contact with a miscarried fetus resulted in the same degree of ritual defilement as contact with any other human body.

It might be noted that the laws of mourning do not apply to a miscarriage. Then again, neither are they applicable to a child who does not survive until the thirtieth day.

In Judaism, the life of the mother, a life in

being, is paramount, always takes precedence over the life of the unborn child. If the mother is endangered by her pregnancy, it must be terminated. In such cases, abortion isn't even optional, but mandatory.

Certain rabbinical authorities were liberal in this regard and included threats to the mother's mental health (on the theory that a distraught woman could commit suicide), in addition to her physical well being.

Some Jewish advocates of abortion use this very narrowly defined exception to the defense of fetal life to argue that Judaism countenances abortion on demand. But the Talmudic debate itself, that is to say, the search for exceptions to the rule, proves the generality—that in the overwhelming majority of cases abortion was forbidden. Nowhere in Judaism has abortion ever been permitted for economic reasons, as a matter of convenience, or as a life choice.

Rabbi Jakobovits, who has written extensively on medical ethics, observes: "The destruction of an unborn child is a grave offense, though not murder." The Union of Orthodox Rabbis has resolved: "For Jews, fetal life is inviolate unless continuation of pregnancy poses a serious threat to the life of the mother."

Some Jews interpret Jewish law to conform with their own value systems. Others are more honest. In an article published in the *Los Angeles Times* on 12 September 1991, Dr. George Flesh explained why he no longer performs abortions. His decision was based on both personal experience and religious commitment.

An OB-GYN in the Los Angeles area, Flesh

recalls that early in his practice a couple came to him seeking an abortion. As the woman's cervix was too rigid to properly dilate, he asked them to come back after a week. In the interim, they changed their minds, and seven months later, he delivered their baby. Years later, he played with their son in the pool of the tennis club to which both families belonged. Says Flesh: "I was horrified to think that only a technical obstacle had prevented me from terminating Jeffrey's potential life."

Moreover, as a newly observant Jew, the doctor was determined to live his life in accordance with divine injunctions. "Judaism has become the lens through which I see the world. The *mitzvot*— God's commandments—guided my behavior. But as a religious Jew my desire to fulfill Torah was absurd as long as I performed elective abortions— a clear transgression. . . . I could not draw closer to God. Wrapping myself in *tallit* and *tefillin* meant nothing. The contradiction was too great. My spiritual aspirations were shattering. My intellectual integrity was disintegrating. I had to stop doing abortions."

What about "reproductive rights," "control of one's body," "freedom of choice?" And now for a truly shocking disclosure: these libertarian doctrines have no place in Judaism.

Putting aside the fact that abortion doesn't just affect the mother, Judaism has never recognized an absolute right to do what one chooses with his or her body. Radical autonomy is wholly incompatible with the concept of divine dominion, which constitutes the bedrock of Judaism.

In Judaism, there is no right to commit suicide. There's no right to needlessly imperil one's life. There is no right to amputate a healthy limb. Even such minor mutilation of the body as tattooing is prohibited by Jewish law.

Regarding the debate over medically assisted suicide (an issue often linked to abortion), Rabbi David Bleich, professor of Talmud and ethics at Yeshiva University, declares: "Autonomy does not extend to one's own life. Man's body and life is the property of the Creator."

When we say *ha'motzi* (the blessing over bread), we thank God for "bringing forth bread from the earth." Why? We—that is to say, man—tilled the soil, planted the seed, irrigated the land, harvested the crops, etc. Why thank Him for that which man hath wrought? But did we make the seed? Did we create the waters of the Earth? Did we place the sun in the heavens? In the final analysis, all life comes not from us but from Him.

From the union of a man and a woman, a child results. The woman wants to control her body. The man wants to control his procreative processes. (Would that they'd thought of this before the interaction occurred.) But neither is ultimately responsible for this new life. The meeting of his sperm and her ovum set the process in motion. But he didn't create his seed, nor she her egg, any more than they fashioned the moon and the stars, the flowers and the trees. At most, men and women can facilitate creation. As the power to generate life is beyond us—in most circumstances—so should be the ability to destroy life.

It's not that individual rights have no place in Judaism, or that liberty is a meaningless concept. Both are important, but only in the proper context. Indeed, Judaism originated the idea of inalienable (that is, God-given) rights. The books of Leviticus and Deuteronomy are filled with injunctions protecting a person's life, liberty, and property. In recognition thereof, our colonial forefathers (who were philo-Semites) chose an inscription from Leviticus for Philadelphia's Liberty Bell: "Proclaim Liberty throughout the land, unto all the inhabitants thereof."

But obligations also are spelled out in considerable detail. For instance, an individual has a right to the product of his labor. Yet coexistent with this right are obligations: not to exploit his workers or even his farm animals, to be honest in his business dealings, to give a portion of his income to the poor, to contribute to the support of the priesthood (or its modern equivalent, the synagogue) and the community. Only in late twentieth century America have we managed to divorce the concept of rights from duties, to sanctify the former while largely ignoring the latter.

An obvious question now arises: Does Jewish law have any bearing on the non-Jewish world? Judaism holds that most of the Torah was given to the Jews alone. Thus while Jews are obligated to keep the dietary laws, to hallow the Sabbath, to pray three times a day in the specified manner, gentiles are under no similar obligations.

There are, however, certain basic moral laws which are incumbent on all of humanity, without which civilization would be impossible. After the flood, the Torah tells us, seven commandments were given to Noah and his progeny—known as the Noahide laws. As we all are descendants of Noah, all of us are bound by these mandates, which include prohibitions against murder, robbery, and sexual immorality, as well as the requirement to establish courts of justice.

Talmudic sages believed this code includes a ban on abortion. Rabbi Yishmoel, a leading authority, interpreted Genesis 9:6 as follows: "Whoever shall spill the blood of human in human, shall his blood be spilled." "Human in human" is the unborn child in its mother's womb, the rabbis reasoned. Rabbi Moses Ben Maimon, known to the world as Maimonides, the great philosopher and medieval codifier of Jewish law, endorsed this interpretation.

So we can see that absent other pressing considerations, Judaism views the protection of fetal life as a universal moral imperative.

Augudath Israel is an influential orthodox social service/lobbying organization. Explaining the group's involvement in the abortion debate (It filed an *amicus* brief in the *Webster* case in favor of overturning *Roe v. Wade*), attorney Chaim Dovid Zwiebel writes: "Although it is not [Agudath Israel's] objective to impose Torah views upon society at large through secular governmental processes, there are certain fundamental values—all of which concededly emanate from Torah—that form the basis of any civilized society. Respect for life is one of them. History has taught that a society in which the dominant theme is 'anything goes' is a society that bears within it the seeds of decay and self-destruction."

As all of life is interconnected, a grand continuum, the decision to allow the destruction of life at one stage has profound repercussions. Today those shock waves are felt in the debate over euthanasia, doctor-assisted suicide, and infanticide. Not surprisingly, Washington state, the only state to legalize abortion by referendum (three years before *Roe v. Wade*), was chosen by right-to-die advocates as a test case for legalized suicide. Just last week, Washington voters narrowly rejected a measure which would have made their state the first jurisdiction in the world to legalize medical murder.

Rabbi Jakobovits, himself a refugee from Nazi Germany, comments: "Once any human being becomes worthless or expendable, all are reduced from an absolute to a relative value and no two human beings would be of equal worth, thus demolishing the very foundation of moral order." And so we have done. And so we are doing. All in the name of freedom and choice.

And thus we return to our starting point: the Jewish mission to humanity. In many ways, the Torah Jew in contemporary America confronts a society not so very different from the pagan world his ancestors challenged and ultimately conquered: a world where violence and brutality are exalted in the entertainment media, then reenacted in our streets; a world of sensual license, where people vie with each other to plumb the depths of depravity; a culture in which the world-weary numb their senses with drugs, where excrement is celebrated as art. Feticide—the wanton destruction of 1.5 million unborn children a year in this country—could well be considered the modern equivalent of pagan sacrifice, a burnt offering to the voracious gods of modernity: radical autonomy, gender sameness, sexual liberation. Overturning these idols is a task worthy of a modern Elijah.

As time goes by, the hazards of an anti-life ethic become increasing apparent. By devaluing life—the life of the unborn, the elderly, the comatose patient, the handicapped—we are, quite literally, digging our own graves.

In one of the most moving passages of the

Torah (Deuteronomy 30:19), the Master of the Universe (blessed be His name) having given Israel his law, tells them that these commandments are the way to life—a life of holiness, justice, and contentment—the only life worthy of the name, as well as the inevitable alternative. "I have set life and death before you this day, blessing and curse. Therefore, choose life, so that you may live—you and your descendants." And let us say: *amen*.

TWELVE

Feminism

Sexual harassment as weapon
(14 October 1991)

Like an avenging angel, Rep. Pat Shroeder (D-Colorado), at the head of a harpy horde, stormed the Senate on the day last week when that citadel of male privilege was scheduled to vote on the Thomas nomination.

How dare they discount the charges of Anita Hill. We demand yet another congressional inquisition (lights, cameras, baseless charges), the feminists fumed.

As for the accuser, who could fail to find her story credible? Hill was so traumatized by Thomas' sexually suggestive remarks that she followed him from one job to another, so brutalized that she asked for a letter of recommendation, so anguished that she invited him to address her law school class, so humiliated that she called him a dozen times (over six years), congratulating him on his marriage, seeking his aid with grant applications. Clearly, here is a woman reduced to trembling terror by a monster's obscene advances.

Why did it take a decade for the story to come out? Hill's defenders have a ready response: Wouldn't any woman be reluctant to come forward, knowing that her suffering will be trivialized and her character impugned? In other words, the more fantastic the allegation, the more it must be believed, else we are guilty of blaming the victim.

On Friday came the latest exquisitely orchestrated revelation: A charge by a woman (with a predilection for sexual harassment suits) Thomas had fired from the EEOC, claiming he made "unwelcome and inappropriate remarks" when she worked for him.

So Thomas goes down in flames, destroyed by an unanswerable accusation (how does one prove what he didn't say in private conversations a decade ago?), and the sexual harassment hysteria grows.

The definition is so vague as to cover almost any conduct, however innocent. Sexual harassment "could be touching, patting, suggestive remarks, verbal abuse, staring, leering, demands for sexual favors or assault," a spokesman for the organization 9 to 5 discloses.

A look is harassment? What kind of look? A longing look, a come-hither glance, a shy smile? For heaven's sake, don't grin at a co-worker of the opposite sex. You'll be hauled before the EEOC in chains.

The feminist position seems to be: A woman has a right to decide, anytime in her life, that anything that ever happened to her was sexual harassment.

Geraldine Ferraro, who lost the woman's vote in 1984, made her own bid for the coveted victim status. It seems that as a young secretary she was harassed by her boss. "He used to stand behind me, very close, and jiggle his money." Little did we realize that Captain Queeg, with his ball bearings, must have been coming on to the crew of the Caine. No wonder they mutinied!

Some women want to see men walking around in a perpetual state of terror, afraid to make eye contact, weighing each word before it's spoken (to assure that it's innuendo-free and couldn't possibly be misinterpreted), flattening themselves against a wall when a woman passes them in a corridor, lest shoulders brush inadvertently.

It's the feminist way of punishing men for everything from diapers to date rape and establishing gender superiority. Not to mention the political capital that can be made from such charges. Even now the National Women's Political Caucus is planning to exploit this latest instance of male insensitivity, to browbeat Congress into passing parental leave and quota legislation.

Several years ago, a friend (we'll call him Ben) was a young associate in a law firm. One day he left a note for his secretary on top of a stack of legal papers. "Barbara, light of my life, fire of my loins (a line from *Lolita*), please file these." As she and Ben were chummy, Barbara was mildly amused.

Another associate, a woman, spied the communication and experienced emotional meltdown, instructing Barbara that she most certainly had been victimized and demanding that she file charges. When Barbara refused, the associate did so herself. An investigation followed. Barbara was called before the partners' committee, asked if she'd like a transfer. She replied that she just wanted to continue working with Ben and to be left in peace. Under no circumstances did she wish to work for a woman lawyer, she added, as she found them intolerably overbearing and intrusive.

Imagine having your career ruined by a casual comment, a glance, a note written in jest? If they can get a Supreme Court nominee, who's safe?

Normal women treat this exaggerated controversy with the contempt it deserves. They don't feel abused, oppressed, or exploited. They don't hate their nature. They do not nurture a gender grudge the size of Mt. Rushmore. They generally like men. If one steps out of line, they know exactly how to handle him. In the feminist-fomented war of the sexes, they are conscientious objectors.

Of families, feminists, and the first lady
(13 May 1990)

Mother's Day reflections on families, feminists, and first ladies:

A throng of twits (twitesses?), approximately 15 percent of the student body of elite Wellesley College, signed a petition protesting the selection of Barbara Bush as this year's commencement speaker.

Make no mistake about it, they are "outraged." Wellesley has taught us that women should be rewarded for their own achievements. But in honoring Barbara Bush, we are recognizing a woman who gained prominence through her husband's exploits, the budding feminists squawked.

No, we certainly don't want women coasting on the accomplishments of their menfolk. But how many of the Wellesley protesters are attending the college of their choice—at an annual cost of $20,000—due to daddy's beneficence? And how many, clutching diplomas in their hot little hands, will find employment (based on merit alone, mind you) in daddy's business? To top it all off, they'll drive to work in their graduation present, a gift from—guess who?

Wellesley has taught them to deprecate the very serious job of mother and homemaker. In reality, honoring the first lady for her husband's achievements makes perfect sense.

Most prominent, married men owe their success in no small part to the behind-the-scenes heroism of their wives. Few men who don't marry ever attain the upper echelons of business, industry, or government.

Wellesley President Nan Keohane told the *New York Times*: "Feminism is very hard to pin down, but it is certainly not anti-family," a comment that certainly qualifies her to be the guest host for "Saturday Night Live."

Stuff and bother. Opposition to the traditional family is the movement's hallmark. As author George Gilder explains: "The family depends on sex roles and feminism, if it is anything, is opposed to sex roles."

From Simone de Beauvoir, who characterized the family as an "obscene bourgeois institution" in *The Second Sex*, to Betty Friedan, who celebrated the proletarian drudgery of Soviet women in *The Feminine Mystiques*, to Gloria Steinem, who has located the origins of marriage in the urge to restrict the freedom of women and perceives the homemaker as a pathological case study in "depression, illness, tension-related diseases, alcoholism, drug addiction and violence," feminist rhetoric is obsessively consistent.

Psychologist Phyllis Chesler, quoted in the *Times* piece, is appalled by those Wellesley women who have managed to transcend indoctrination in their desire to hear Mrs. Bush. "Many women still want to live in a castle, still believe in the myth of rescue by marriage and still believe in Prince Charming," Chesler sadly observes. This from the lady who wrote *Women and Madness*, which argued that marriage literally drives women nuts. Not anti-family, did you say?

These attitudes suffuse women's studies programs—which Gilder terms "the most brutal brainwashing since Joseph Stalin introduced compulsory nursery school in the Soviet Union"—from lectures to textbooks to assigned reading.

While women's studies may be the most extreme instance, this cultural indoctrination is pervasive. The mass media eulogize career women and denigrate those who choose to devote themselves to life's most important task (nurturing the next generation).

Donna Reed and Jane Wyatt were Fifties stereotypes. Today, television glamorizes career women on such programs as "L.A. Law," "Murphy Brown," and "Who's the Boss," while virtually ignoring the majority of women with preschool children who choose employment in the home.

Barbara Bush offends the Wellesley protesters precisely because she is the incarnate refutation of their mind-set: a woman whose success was based on her decision to forgo college and career in favor of full-time mothering. Despite their protestations that they want women to have more options, they revile those who make the ideologically incorrect choice.

What price women in combat
(22 June 1992)

For women in combat, rape by the enemy should be considered an "occupational hazard." That was only the most bizarre comment coming out of recent testimony before the presidential commission studying the ban on sending women into battle.

Republican administrations have no idea of how the game is played. You're supposed to appoint a commission which will ratify the foreordained conclusion, thus allowing the president to say: "Gosh, I guess I'll just have to go along with the recommendations of my blue ribbon panel."

This particular commission is loaded with retired generals and admirals. Clearly the Bush White House thinks military men, hard-headed pragmatists that they are, will take a realistic approach. In fact, the military is like any other bureaucracy, prone to the same conventional wisdom and uncritical thinking.

The scrambled eggheads on the commission took the P.C. party line, with questions implying that there are no discernible differences between the sexes when it comes to martial skills. As if the army didn't have different physical performance standards for men and women. As if West Point didn't have cadets running in effete little jogging shoes instead of combat boots, training with Tonka-toy rifles, to accommodate women.

Yes, the military has gone out of its way to adapt to the prevailing cultural orthodoxy. The Gulf War was over for sixteen months before we learned that at least one of our POWs was raped.

Testifying before the commission, Major Rhonda Cornum, who was captured after her helicopter was shot down over Iraq, at first maintained that she was "treated exactly the same" as male prisoners. Under questioning from Commissioner Elaine Donnelly, Cornum admitted that she was "violated manually, vaginally and rectally" by her captors. As almost an afterthought, the major added that such treatment was "an occupational hazard of going to war."

Did you get that, Middle America? If your wives or daughters are drafted and raped as prisoners—well, that just goes with the territory.

There's no draft now. But what guarantees can they give us that it won't be reinstituted? And what assurances will we have that if women are allowed in combat, they won't be drafted *into* combat as well?

Currently, women are exempt from draft registration. A 1981 Supreme Court decision upholding the exemption made the connection between it and the ban on women in combat. "The purpose of registration was to prepare for a draft of combat troops. Since women are excluded from combat, Congress concluded that they would not be needed in the event of a draft, and therefore decided not to register them." Once the exclusion is removed, the exemption must fall.

The commission also heard testimony on the

Air Force's SERE (Survival, Evasion, Resistance, and Escape) program, where trainees undergo simulated interrogation and torture. They discovered that while women held up as well as men, the latter were intensely affected by the screams of women. There was concern that male POWs might do anything to keep women soldiers from being abused.

The military's answer—desensitize the men, condition them to the anguished cries of women. But if current reports are accurate, the services have a serious problem with sexual harassment. A week before the hearings, seventy naval aviators were implicated in the Tailhook convention scandal, where airmen flying on 90-proof fumes allegedly groped any woman they could lay boozy hands on. The solution—sensitize the savages. The Navy has started a servicewide program to combat sexual exploitation.

Thus servicemen will be alternately sensitized and desensitized, instructed to treat women with deference, then taught to regard them as one of the guys. As if emotions can be turned on and off, like tap water.

Many of our most troublesome social problems (from wife/girlfriend beating to family desertion) stem from the triumph of the feminist dogma of gender fungibility. Men were told that women are no different than they. Some acted accordingly.

At their invitation, I too testified before the commission. I told the assembled brass hats that, if required, I would give my life's blood for this country. If my two sons were called to service in time of war, I would send them forth with great trepidation. If my daughters were going to be placed in a situation where they could be subjected to the horrors so blithely described by Major Cornum, I would urge them to head for Canada.

Men's movement hears a trendy beat
(27 June 1991)

Okay men, here's what we're gonna do: This weekend we're going to beat drums in the woods, abuse our epidermal layers in an Indian sweat lodge, and rediscover the warrior within us.

You see, we've been oppressed by society, turned into "success objects," who are valued for our incomes alone. Having been sold a masculine mystique (which defines masculinity in terms of "efficiency, autonomy and inhuman power"), we are in spiritual crisis.

The industrial revolution severed our roots, took us from a man's work on the land—grubbing turnips in the field with our sons—depriving us of the opportunity for backbreaking, fourteen-hour-a-day labor and a forty-year life span.

So we gotta get our consciousness raised, devise our own rites of passage, and learn to express our grief.

The cover story in the June 24 *Newsweek* ("Drums, Sweat and Tears: What Do Men Really Want") heralds the men's movement. "What teenagers were to the 1960s, what women were to the 1970s, middle-aged men will be to the 1990s: America's sanctioned grievance carriers," the magazine muses. In our persecution-fetish culture, if you ain't a victim, you ain't nothing, baby.

"There are hundreds of men's groups around

the country." Those on a gender identity trip are spending $250 for a weekend of tom-tom thumping, spiritually invigorating sweats, and fireside therapy (pain sharing).

"Men have found a weekend retreat to be a profoundly moving and impressive experience," the magazine discloses. One of the accompanying photos shows a group of mustachioed dudes, bandannas wrapped around their heads, clutching sticks, looking for all the world like accountants who stumbled onto the set of *Deliverance*.

You don't believe we're oppressed? Just look at the statistics, my friend. We have a premature death rate 40 percent higher than that of women. Men dominate the prison population, *Newsweek* informs us in the hushed tones of revelation. Odd, I had assumed all of those rapes, armed robberies, and triple-ax murders were committed by Avon ladies on crack.

Absurdity begets absurdity. Why should women be the only ones to make fools of themselves with oppression fantasies? We need equal opportunity persecution complexes.

And what is a movement without a political program? Holding forth in the *New York Times*, Andrew Kimbrell, identified as a lawyer and environmentalist who writes frequently about "men's issues," offers an Alan Alda agenda.

As our movement matures, it will advance a program to help men, "re-establish ties with . . . their families, communities and the earth." As we recover an "inner sense of wildness," we'll call for more environmental protection. A renewed commitment to home and hearth will act as an impetus for parental leave legislation. As we come to reject "modern techno-war [that] mocks the inner warrior aspect of men," we'll turn our backs on militarism. In other words, we will confirm our masculinity (hug the hairy-chested, rampaging brute within us) by becoming eco-freaks, pacifists, and house husbands.

The movement scorns the flaccid, sensitive, new man—who achieves an ecstatic state flagellating himself over "violence to women"—activists are quick to assure us. But their prophet, Robert Bly, is a wimpy, white-haired poet, who looks like a septuagenarian Wally Cox. Bit of a Conan credibility gap here. If Bly is its captain, Richard Simmons must be the movement's icon.

Poor, pathetic castraltos, psychologically emasculated by feminism. The only way they can respond to gender intimidation is with a movement of their own: hollow rituals, pseudo-solidarity, blubbering kids playing Indians in the woods. They haven't an inkling of what masculinity is really about.

Paradoxically, men discover who they are, not in the company of other men, but only with women. The little lost boys who spend their evenings carousing with the guys are doomed to eternal adolescence.

A man is fulfilled not in woodsy solitude or urban debauches but with a wife and family, who will satisfy the most profoundly masculine drive—the urge to serve and protect.

The most masculine man I know always came home to his wife and son after a hard day's work. He never hit me and rarely raised his voice. He taught me to be truthful, diligent, and respect the gentler sex—in short, to be a man.

We should celebrate not the savage but the civilized male. Our society is plagued by a super-abundance of psychic warriors, males who pamper the inner barbarian, who can express their manhood only in meaningless rites: booze, drugs, violence, and transient sex.

Divorce, family dissolution, efforts to eradicate sexual identity aggravate the savage inclinations of nomadic males. Neither their wildness nor the loneliness of middle-aged men deprived of families will be solved by the farce of boys trying to assert their masculinity by playing Chingachgook, to the beat, beat, beat of the trendy drums.

THIRTEEN

Culture

Too many rights will kill us
(22 August 1991)

Opponents of Clarence Thomas believe they've found the ultimate weapon—the political equivalent of Darth Vader's Death Star.

Last week, the Senate Judiciary Committee released a series of incriminating documents: Thomas' speeches, lists of video rentals, baseball cards. Buried in the mass of documentation was a 1988 address to the Pacific Institute, wherein the nominee expressed grave doubts about our enshrinement of the rights concept.

"Too great an emphasis on economic rights distorts the principles of good government," Thomas told the libertarian think-tank. "In fact, too great an emphasis on rights can be harmful for democracy."

Forget the date of Mother's Day. Forgo a second helping of apple pie. Make rude remarks about the American flag, but do not—repeat, do not—doubt the truth and beauty of rights-mania. At the mere mention of the magic word, we are all expected to assume a beatific expression and *sa-*

217

laam three times toward the ACLU's national head-quarters.

I liked Judge Thomas from the outset, and my esteem for him grows with each revelation. I'll go him one better: An obsession with individual rights is destroying our society.

To voice concern about the current rights proliferation is not to deny the importance of fundamental freedoms. Most of us have ancestors who hailed from lands where common people were chattels of the elite. My maternal grandfather came from a country where he couldn't vote, own land, obtain an education, or pursue most vocations. He was, however, afforded the delightful opportunity of serving in the army for twenty-five years, a privilege he declined by emigrating.

People who come from that background don't have to be told that without certain liberties, life is barely worth living. In the twentieth century, examples abound of regimes that have reduced their subjects to the status of domesticated animals, where daily existence is a gray grind. In the People's Detention Center of China, it is now a crime to wear T-shirts with pessimistic slogans.

But an excess of any good thing (food, water, even air) can kill you. The manufacture of spurious rights, of rights severed from responsibilities, is tearing our nation apart. Rights are goodies doled out by our mother state. Rights have become entitlements, the enforcement of which benefits one group as it bloodies another.

• NEA-subsidized artists demand their right to shock and offend, at our expense—a collect, obscene phone call.

• The networks have a right to pollute the

airwaves with obscenity and sexual suggestiveness, promote promiscuity, and attack religion. Hollywood has a right to produce lurid fare that causes riots in theaters and feeds sick psyches. Syncopated savages have a right to set their fantasies to music, to croon their gentle invitations to date rape at concerts.

• The homeless have a right to urinate in public, turn bus stations into vacation condominiums, and harass subway riders for spare change.

• Doctors with AIDS have a right to privacy, even at the cost of patients' lives. Addicts have a right to "treatment on demand."

• Then there's Harvard Law professor Alan Dershowitz—the man who practically wrote the Bill of Rights—who declares that Pee Wee Herman had a right to (*ahem*) become romantically involved with himself in a porno theater. Life, liberty, and the pursuit of orgasm.

Like bawling brats, we petulantly demand our imagined rights, not from any disinterested commitment to principle but because we believe life owes us (plenty): "I gotta right to a job!" "I gotta right to have my sexual preference validated!" "I gotta right to control my body, or to have the consequences of a lack of self-control disposed of conveniently."

Absent a delicate balance—rights and duties, freedom and order—the social fabric begins to unravel. The rights explosion of the past three decades has taken us on a rapid descent to a culture without civility, decency, or even that degree of discipline necessary to maintain an advanced industrial civilization. Our cities are cesspools, our urban schools terrorist training camps, our legislatures brothels where rights are sold to the highest electoral bidder.

Current rights inflation could eventually lead to the demise of liberty. People can't exist indefinitely in a state of near anarchy. Democracy in the streets—spiraling violence, group warfare with the property of the toiling classes as spoils—ends with the advent of jackbooted legions. The license of Weimar Germany was midwife to the repression of the Third Reich.

I believe Clarence Thomas understands this. A Supreme Court justice who affirms that rights don't exist in a vacuum, that none is absolute and all ideally serve a higher purpose, who dares to inquire as to the consequences of proposed rights, is an exciting prospect.

America loses its work ethic
(6 April 1992)

Hard times breed economic quackery. The Buy American bandwagon is large enough to accommodate loose nuts of every variety.

Lloyd D. Paine of Jamul, California, writes to enlist my support in his Buy American National Campaign. "Will we heed the warning signs and wake up to what is happening all around us, the loss of jobs and industry. . . ?" Lloyd theatrically inquires. If so, we must embrace the obvious solution to our predicament: "getting the American consumer to look first at American goods and services. . . ."

The campaign will bestow a "gold seal of approval" on those patriotic products made with "100 percent American parts and labor" and silver seals on merchandise of at least 70 percent purity. Those unfortunate items whose composition is contaminated in excess of 30 percent would remain seal-less.

Such silly commercial chauvinism aside, America's industrial decline is no laughing matter. My real objection to the Buy American frenzy is that it distracts us from the underlying problem. That U.S. products have fallen out of favor with both foreigners and Americans is symptomatic of the virtual disappearance of the work ethic in this country.

Consider the following (then try to convince yourself it's all a MITI—Japanese international trade ministry—conspiracy): Among the top ten models in J.D. Power and Associates 1991 auto ratings, only one (No. 8) was American.

Japan is pulling a 46 percent market share of U.S. car buyers under age forty-five. In 1960, we manufactured 75 percent of the world's cars. We now make 25 percent. In 1965, we produced 27 percent of the world's exports; the Japanese 7 percent. Since then, our share has fallen 7 percentage points, theirs has risen by the same amount.

Between 1960 and 1973, U.S. productivity for non-agricultural workers increased an average of 2.9 percent a year. After 1973, it grew at an annual rate of less than 1 percent.

To understand these disastrous trends, you could do no better than to read a slender volume by Chuck Colson and Jack Eckerd: *Why America Doesn't Work*.

The authors trace the productivity slump to the demise of the work ethic, itself a result of a loss of faith. The men who built this country (who settled our shores, farmed the land, worked the

factories and mines), no less than those who built
the great cathedrals of Europe, believed they were
doing God's work.

In the beginning, God created, Genesis tells
us. In imitation of Him, man is called upon to
work and by his effort complete creation. Work
gets favorable mention in the Ten Commandments
("Six days shall you labor and do all of your
work. . . .") "It is good and proper for a man . . .
to accept his lot and be happy in his work—this is
a gift of God," Ecclesiastes instructs.

This Jewish doctrine was a radical departure
from the pagan perspective. The Greeks and Romans viewed work as contemptible, demeaning to
the man of culture and refinement, fit only for
slaves. By ennobling work, first Judaism and then
Christianity taught people to value what they did
more than their social status.

Our founding fathers were imbued with this
spirit, the authors note. "Choose that employment
or calling in which you may be most serviceable to
God," exhorted Puritan writer Richard Baxter.
"Choose not that in which you may be most rich
or honorable . . . but that in which you may do
most good. . . ." Or, as my immigrant grandfather, a tailor, used to say: A man should never be
ashamed of honest work, however menial.

Under the skeptical, modernist impulse, we
lost the work ethic early in this century. Like a
plant whose roots are severed, America continued
to thrive for a few decades longer, carried along
by momentum. (We knew work was good, but
forgot why.) Then came the Sixties and a general
questioning of values, a pervasive dissatisfaction
with lots in life.

It's often wondered how the hippies of the Sixties could have become the yuppies of the Eighties. No contradiction here, say Colson and Eckerd. The former merely took the ethos forged in the crucible of revolution (live for the moment, crude materialism) and applied it to the workplace.

This gave us two extremes: the relentless pursuit of leisure and the workaholic—work for its own sake. Among collars of all colors (white and blue alike), cynicism is pandemic—what's-in-it-for-me replacing loyalty to employer, pride in workmanship, and application as an expression of transcendent values. In a recent survey, only 16 percent said they were doing the best job they could.

Instead of buying American, we'd be better off buying back into the value system that made American goods worth buying in the first place.

Summer of Love worth forgetting
(12 August 1987)

In case you missed it, and I certainly wish I had, this is the twentieth anniversary of the so-called Summer of Love.

During the dog days of 1967, hippies, yippies, and all manner of transcendental tourists flocked to our funkier urban areas—Haight-Ashbury in San Francisco, New York's Greenwich Village, and Cambridge's Harvard Square—to do their tiresome thing.

Now a bunch of wilting ex-flower children (headbands circling their graying locks) are getting teary-eyed reminiscing over their moment in the psychedelic sun.

The occasion has loosened an avalanche of

books and magazine articles. San Francisco is spon-
soring a series of commemorative events throughout the summer, capped with a concert and rally
at Golden Gate Park on September 21.

Lest this flood of nostalgia wash away the
modicum of normalcy restored in the past two
decades, it is well to reflect on what the era really
was about.

The 1960s were the highwater mark of half-a-
century of nihilism and irrationality in American
culture. Its themes were immaturity, self-indulgence, and the substitution of slogans for ideas.
Consider the distinguishing characteristics of
Aquarian society.

LOVE—Love was the password. It was ubiquitous, with love-ins, love children, free love, and of
course the summer of love. Luckily, most of this
passion could be cured with penicillin.

Love-ins, by the way, were not what the designation suggests. There was nothing even vaguely
sexual about these happenings, unless your idea
of the erotic is a gang of dirty, disheveled infants,
wandering around declaring their affinity for all
and sundry, dancing barefooted in muddy fields.

There was, nonetheless, a superfluity of sex
in the Sixties, hollow and ultimately self-destruc-
tive though it might be. Those who indiscriminately declared their love for humanity, who were
ready to copulate at the drop of a pair of bell-
bottom jeans, seemed incapable of feeling loyalty
or affection for specific individuals. The outlook
was summed up by a popular T-shirt slogan: "I
love humanity; it's people I can't stand."

DRUGS—Drugs were the pervasive motif.
They shaped the era's music and art, even perme-

ated its lexicon, in such expressions as *bad trip*, *bummer, far out*, and *blow your mind*.

It was the first rebellion in history fueled not by principles but chemical substances. It's ironic that the rebels were considered youthful idealists. Drug addiction isn't the emblem of idealism, but proof of its absence.

The drug culture underwent an inevitable progression. Trips turned bad. Kids killed themselves leaping from buildings. While dealers fought bloody turf wars, novice junkies graduated from LSD and pot to coke and heroin. The do-it-if-it-feels-good mentality of the age survives in epidemic rates of adolescent substance abuse.

MUSIC—This syncopated noise—discordant, chaotic clatter meant to blot out consciousness—was well-suited to a vegetative existence. It was as if the kids were afraid to be alone with their thoughts, for even a moment, and needed a constant barrage of soul-jarring sound (an auditory drug) to numb the senses.

There was a subliminal violence to acid rock—the savage beat of the sensual jungle, an expression of dark, erotic forces waiting to burst the constraints of civilization.

RELIGION—Eastern was in. Buddhism, Zen, anything Oriental. Gurus garnered disciples and established ashrams. Youth who found the faith they were raised in suffocating had no difficulty swallowing the most bizarre buncombe: astrology, ESP, reincarnation. It was the age of credulity.

POLITICS—Western democracy was too repressive; totalitarianism was groovy. The generation's political heroes were cynical demagogues—Mao, Ho, and Che—who preached gun-barrel power and class genocide.

Flower children bequeathed to the people of Southeast Asia regimes devoid of even a hint of humanity.

As memory dims, myths grow. There was nothing particularly idealistic, heroic, or compassionate about the era's institutions and cultural manifestations. A big chill runs down my spine just thinking of how close to the abyss we came during the Sixties. If there was anything even remotely resembling love in this travesty, I'll take acrimony every time.

Education "hand writeing" is on the wall
(22 February 1990)

H. Joachim Maitre, dean of the Boston University College of Communications, has an amusing anecdote, the punch line of which is apropos to the subject at hand.

It seems the nineteenth-century Austro-Hungarian Emperor Joseph had to sit through a two-hour opening session of parliament. At the conclusion, his majesty, then in his eighties, shuffled to the podium and uttered a single sentence in Latin: *Totus mundis stultizat*—the whole world is growing stupid.

Regrettably, the emperor neglected to offer an explanation for this phenomenon. But those acquainted with the American educational system know the answer.

I am in receipt of a letter from a young man objecting to a recent column on affirmative action in college admissions. What is significant here isn't his views, but his pathetic inability to express them intelligibly.

My correspondent wonders rhetorically how I could write "such a *(sic)* article such as this one in this day in *(sic)* age." He consistently uses "their" when he wants "there." In his vocabulary, "nonverbal," "mainstream," and "yourself" all are two words. Counsel, as in legal counsel, is spelled "council." The writer urges me to tell the "hole truth." Is this the truth about black holes or pot-holes?

Dependent clauses are offered as complete sentences. His run on sentences and inarticulate attempts at expression defy description. Consider the following: "Their *(sic)* are often times people who do abuse the system, but you make it seem that all Black *(sic)* and minority groups are the only ones who are on Welfare *(sic)*, when in fact more just as many and even more so White *(sic)* people are on welfare." Sick.

The author of this travesty isn't a grade school dropout or a bilingual education student, but a college junior, majoring in political science. His illiteracy is no way exceptional.

In 1986, the National Assessment of Educational Progress released the results of an exhaustive survey of the writing ability of 55,000 students in the fourth, eighth, and eleventh grades. Among the findings: Fewer than one in four college-bound students writes well enough to succeed at higher education or future employment.

Of the eleventh-graders, less than 25 percent could handle the simplest analytical writing assignment. Fewer than a third could expound their ideas on paper.

Despite a massive increase in education spending during the Reagan years, the situation has not improved in the interim. Last year, Education Secretary Lauro Cavazos pronounced the nation's school system stagnant. Boston University President John Silber, currently on leave while campaigning for governor of Massachusetts, said it all: "What a high-school diploma tells you is that a student was *institutionalized* for about 12 years. You wouldn't know whether the student had been in a prison colony, a reform school or a place for mental defectives."

Much the same could be said of college education. In his book *The Irrelevant English Teacher*, J. Mitchell Morse reproduces the writing samples of college English majors. (Please welcome America's future educators.) "She was pure as a vestigial virgin," wrote one scholar who had obviously confused anatomy with theology, while another disclosed that "Chaucer was the greatest middle-aged writer." Yet another urged: "In are *(sic)* times the responcable *(sic)* writers must read the hand writeing *(sic)* on the wall so he can asses *(sic)* the human conditions." The "hand writeing" is indeed on the wall, in depressingly large script.

Back to my correspondent, the product of twelve years of public school and three years of college education. Presumably, each of his English teachers gave him a passing grade, his grammatical depravity notwithstanding.

How did this benighted young man pass his freshman composition class? Was his instructor merely lazy, afraid to fail him, or as ignorant as he?

I recall that in my freshman composition class, R.W. Pence (a pedagogic drill sergeant) returned one paper seven times for corrections. But the R.W.

Pences of higher education are ancient history. Today colleges are too busy indoctrinating, raising social consciousness and eliminating Western bias in curriculums to bother with such mundane matters as teaching their charges to express themselves coherently in their mother tongue.

Public education is hopeless. As with other socialist institutions, reform is impossible. A society with even a minimal survival instinct would be moving as quickly as possible toward private schooling. Instead, Republicans and Democrats, liberals and conservatives alike pledge their allegiance to our illiteracy factories.

As for my correspondent, he is an academic double-amputee, the victim of educational malpractice. Worst of all, he probably considers himself exceptionally well-educated, a veritable renaissance man. When he enters the workforce, where writing skills are essential for management, he is in for a rude awakening. Then again, in light of his major, if he can't hold down a clerical position, he can always serve in Congress and work for an increase in educational expenditures. Emperor Joseph was a prophet.

Cultures: They're not created equal
(16 April 1992)

Last week's news that Dartmouth College is expanding its Third World educational requirement reminded me of a recent adventure in multicultural land with a prominent Mad Hatter.

I had just finished taping a TV show on multiculturalism and was leaving the studio when I encountered the local leader of a mainline civil rights group, who was waiting to do another segment. As we were shaking hands he inquired if I knew there were Jews in Columbus' crew? (Ol' Chris' name had come up in the course of the program.)

I replied that I'd heard there were Marranos (Jews forced to convert during the Inquisition) on the venerable voyage. No, no, these were *Moorish* (black) Jews, the activist interjected. And was I further apprised that the "original Jews" were black?

I thought perhaps I'd misunderstood him. I knew there were black Jews from Ethiopia, I said. But surely he wasn't suggesting that Abraham, Isaac, and Jacob were black? That was precisely his point.

Said the White Queen in *Alice*: "When I was young I practiced believing three impossible things before breakfast. Now I can believe anything."

I was tempted to say something cheeky like, "Yes, I'd heard that Cecil B. DeMille wanted to cast Sidney Poitier as Moses in *The Ten Commandments*," but merely smiled, thanked him for the information, and departed. What does one say to a man in the grip of a delusion?

This compulsion to expropriate other people's cultures is just one aspect of the assault on Western civilization which goes by the misleading moniker multiculturalism.

Fantasy histories aside, there's nothing wrong with studying other cultures. But is it too much to ask that children first learn about their own, to give them a basis for comparison? When the National Endowment for the Humanities tells us that 68 percent of high school seniors don't know when the Civil War occurred, two-thirds can't identify

the Reformation and Magna Carta, and 64 percent can't name the author of *The Canterbury Tales*,
clearly our schools are failing their primary function.

The mummery of multicultural shamans notwithstanding, we do have a common culture in
this country, based on shared ideas developed first
in the civilizations of antiquity, later matured in
Western Europe.

Our political traditions come from English
common law, not the Iroquois federation. Our
ethics come from the Bible, not the sayings of
Confucius. Our aesthetic ideals are derived from
many sources, including Shakespeare, Renaissance
painters, and classical music, not the chants of Ibo
tribesmen and aboriginal cave drawings.

That certain blacks, Hispanics, Orientals, and
Native Americans feel neglected is unfortunate
but irrelevant. In a strictly biological sense, it isn't
my culture either. My great-grandparents weren't
reading Chaucer and listening to Mozart in Czarist Russia.

Those who can't appreciate human greatness
unless it's manifested by their own are sad speci-
mens. Both Clarence Thomas and I are members
of the International Churchill Society. That a
grandson of black sharecroppers and a grandson
of Jewish immigrants each can celebrate a man
who was the quintessence of Victorianism is one
of the wonders of a culture which transcends artificial barriers.

The unstated premise of multiculturalism is
cultural equality or relativism. The very notion
that one culture is superior to another is anath-
ema to adherents of the creed.

Well, beat me with the collected writings of Prof. Leonard Jeffries (the melanin-obsessed academic) and call me a malignant monoculturalist, but I do not for a minute believe that Mandarin society, which crippled women by binding their feet, or Indian society, which burned widows on their husbands' funeral pyres, or Aztec society, which sacrificed virgins by the tens of thousands, are the equivalent of a culture that invented the concept of individual rights, launched the industrial revolution, and doubled the human life span within two centuries.

Cultural relativism is the alter ego of moral relativism. Its implicit message: "You may think that X is wrong, but that's only your white, patriarchal, Judeo-Christian, heterosexist tradition talking. Look at all the cultures that condone X."

Get set for the ultimate in multiculturalism. In December, the "Book-of-the-Month-Club News" offered a volume, *Aztecs*, by British scholar Inga Clendinnen. The author helps us to understand the lives of these "extraordinary people," who engaged in such quaint customs as tearing the hearts out of sacrificial victims, by putting their rites in the proper cultural perspective.

The "News" informs us: "Clendinnen's achievement is that, in explaining how human sacrifice fit into the everyday Aztec worldview, she make the violent pageants and rituals not just understandable, but also *moving and even beautiful.*" But of course, indigenous cultures are always moving and beautiful, especially those displaced by genocidal cultural imperialists like Columbus and his successors.

Ending human sacrifice was Western (Judeo-Christian) civilization's first great achievement.

Multiculturalism is literally turning the moral clock back 3,600 years. Watch out. There may be an Aztec priest in your future.

Rudeness still rules the roost
(14 November 1984)

Time Magazine can sniff out a cultural trend the way a bloodhound tracks a fugitive. The cover story in the November 5 issue informs us that we are "Minding Our Manners Again."

Heroine of the piece is Judith Martin, syndicated columnist, who—as Miss Manners—instructs the uncouth in matters of decorum. Martin's partially tongue-in-cheek column is carried by more than two-hundred newspapers nationwide.

Other evidence of a groundswell of politeness, noted by the magazine, includes a spate of recently published etiquette books. The revised and expanded *Amy Vanderbilt's Complete Book of Etiquette* vies with an updated version of Emily Post's magnum opus for the newly-mannered market.

For corporate social climbers, there's *The New Office Etiquette*. Letitia Baldridge, author of the revised *Vanderbilt* book, offers seminars for young executives seeking refinement (at $6,000 for a full-day course). One entrepreneur of culture even conducts an etiquette course for pre-schoolers ("Petite Protocol") and lectures on table manners for businessmen ("International Dining: Eating Your Way to the Top").

If the news magazine is to be believed, we are approaching the dawn of a gilded age of proper conduct. Not so.

This infatuation with gentility is primarily an upper middle class phenomenon. Yuppies, bored with their pasta machines and parlor games, are aping the customs of a bygone era (not necessarily a bad thing, as almost any age is preferable to our own).

The manners of the clod on the street are still abysmal, and may actually be deteriorating. Take teen-agers—providing you have a strong stomach. These adolescent huns make New York cabbies seem genteel by comparison.

Have you ever held a door for a young lady (term loosely employed) whose response to the courtesy was stony silence? Doubtless the words "thank you" have never escaped her juvenile lips. What of the species—male variety—who, when introduced to a stranger, stares mutely at the floor?

My favorite is the cretin with his 100-megaton radio who feels he must share the discordant sounds emanating therefrom with everyone on a crowded bus. A close runner-up is the oaf who insists on maintaining a loud dialogue with his giggling girlfriend during a movie.

Teen-agers do not have a monopoly on rudeness. (It only seems that way, because they devote so much effort to it.) Urban life presents daily examples of thoughtless behavior: the pompous secretary—whose specialty is long distance intimidation, the waitress who says "have a nice day" with a frown on her face, the cashier who practically throws your change at you, the idiot driver who begins blasting his horn milliseconds after the light changes, and the boobs who jostle you on crowded sidewalks.

Good manners are more than an avenue to

business success or a nostalgic longing for the Victorian age. They are the mortar of tradition which binds our society together. Indeed, social disintegration has paralleled the decline of manners in this century.

The ultimate justification for politeness is self-interest combined with a regard for others. Etiquette makes life infinitely more pleasant. The mad scramble for advantage is replaced by an attitude of *noblesse oblige*; animosity gives way to tolerance.

The essence of etiquette is kindness and consideration. It is all well and good to know which fork to use at dinner and the correct salutation for an ex-ambassador, but knowing when to ask permission, how to express gratitude, and when to defer to another is far more important. It is this which distinguishes the gentleman and lady from the fishwife, the bumpkin and the lout.

The paradigm of unpretentious etiquette was the immigrant of yesterday. He didn't know the rules of urbanity, but did know how to treat the guest in his home. He would have been totally out of place at a dress ball, had someone invited him, but was very much home in a church or synagogue.

The old immigrants dealt honestly in business, showed kindness to strangers and generosity to friends and family. Those who seek refinement would do well to follow their example.

October: A rich spectacle
(7 October 1991)

October is, hands down, my favorite month. There's something to be said for April, when the earth shrugs off its robe of winter slumber, and July, when lushness suffuses the landscape.

Ah, but October is nothing short of grand. Crisp mornings, warm afternoons, cool evenings. What could be more invigorating than the wake-up call of the early morning air in this vintage month?

I speak, of course, of a New England autumn, and why one would want to be anywhere else in October is beyond me. Here in sugar maple country, nature cloaks itself in riotous color. Trees catch fire, blazing with crimson, ocher, and burnished gold.

The autumn, of which October is queen, is a time of new beginnings. Lazy days of sand and suntan lotion are behind us. We shake off summer's doldrums and lay the foundation for future progress. August is the southern hemisphere—easy and indolent. October is northern climes, brisk and busy, infused with a work ethic.

October is a rugged season; none of the simpering softness of spring here. It evokes images of a man in a plaid jacket, trudging home across a barren field in the last light of day, a spaniel at his side; high school gladiators locked in combat on a football field; animals laying on an extra layer of fat for winter hibernation.

October is the taste of mulled cider, the smell of a candle scorching the inside of a jack-o-lantern, the sight of cattails waving in a marsh, of mist rising off a lake, of children joyously flinging themselves on leaf piles, of midget monsters on a confection raid, screaming down darkened streets.

Driving to a dinner one evening in late October, I caught sight of a flock of Canada geese, silhouetted against the moon, elegant creatures on a lonely mission. My heart went out to them. On a gray morning, I passed a white clapboard church, a ladder leaning against its side, its steeple storming heaven. Eternity, it whispered, echoing the month's message.

October is rich in memories; running round the school track your tail toasty as the arctic end of an iceberg, a gym teacher snapping at your heels, feeling warm and woolly in a new argyle sweater; harvest fairs with corn stalks standing sentry over mounds of pumpkins; that aching romance of your freshman college year.

Now kissing a girl in the spring, when girls are shy as daffodils, is fine. And a summer kiss, stolen on a moonlit terrace, has undeniable charm. But to kiss a lass after an October walk, her cheeks cold and flushed, her lips soft and yielding, is to taste love's true elixir.

Why is it that the older I get, the more poignant October becomes? Is it because death stalks October, and its luster is a prelude to the white shroud soon to come? The month is an aging, reckless playboy, knowing it's his last fling. It's as if nature, clinging tenaciously to life, determined to go out in a blaze of glory—a splendid doom.

October is a metaphor for a dying civilization, resplendent in its dotage. America today is October country; brilliant hues, dazzling scenes, frantic activity masking decay, like the bright colors of a leaf pile mingling with the musty odor of dissolution.

At October's close comes Halloween, haunted eve when the world is given over to nightmare creatures. Ghosts, goblins, and ghouls caper about, daring us to refuse them a treat. Our own monsters, all too real—sexual savages gnawing at the nation's moral innards, nihilists masquerading as artists, armies of angry mendicants, posturing politicians only too willing to sell us into slavery for a bag full of votes—will dance on the rubble of civilization. Here are demons, intent on soaping society's windows, who won't be appeased by chocolate bars or candy corn.

Still, like the seasons, civilizations come and go. The passing of one gives nourishment to the next. After October, the world slides into a wintry grave, to await rebirth in the spring. After this life, life eternal beckons us.

October is a wistful time. Soon the rains will come; the wind will bite; the snow will fly. But that knowledge, far from depressing, only enhances our urgent pleasure in the rich spectacle.